Feng Shui

Everything You Need to Know About Feng Shui from Beginner to Expert

Veronica Fujii

Veronica Fujii

Veronica Fujii

Disclaimer Notice:

Please note the information contained within this document is for educational and entertainment purposes only. Every attempt has been made to provide accurate, up to date and reliable, complete information. No warranties of any kind are expressed or implied. Readers acknowledge that the author is not engaging in the rendering of legal, financial, medical or professional advice.

Table of Contents

Introduction 7

Chapter 1: Feng Shui-What and Why? 9

Chapter 2: The Theories of Feng Shui 19

Chapter 3: Getting Started with Feng Shui 29

Chapter 4: Feng Shui Auspicious Symbols and Tokens 39

Chapter 5: Feng Shui Tips for Your Home 75

Chapter 6: Feng Shui Tips for Children's Rooms 81

Chapter 7: Feng Shui Tips for the Garden 89

Chapter 8: Feng Shui Tips for the Bathroom 95

Chapter 9: Feng Shui for a Senior Citizen's Room 99

Chapter 10: Feng Shui Tips for the Garage 103

Chapter 11: Feng Shui Tips for the Office 107

Chapter 12: Feng Shui Tips for the Bedroom 113

Chapter 13: Feng Shui Tips for the Kitchen 117

Chapter 14: Decluttering.. 121

Chapter 15: Feng Shui Tips for the Living Room 127

Chapter 16: The Benefits of Feng Shui 131

Chapter 17: Feng Shui for Stress Relief 143

Chapter 18: Secret Ways to Improve Your Feng Shui 153

Chapter 19: Frequently Asked Questions on Feng Shui.......... 161

Chapter 20: Feng Shui Tips for Beginners 171

Chapter 21: Applying the Elements through Color 181

Chapter 22: Applying the Elements through Shapes 189

Chapter 23: How to Enhance Energy in Feng Shui Corners.... 193

Chapter 24: Feng Shui Tip for Your Purse 203

Conclusion.. 211

Introduction

Thank you for purchasing this book titled, "Feng Shui: Essential Feng Shui Guide For Increased Simplicity, Peace, and Prosperity". We hope this book serves as a comprehensive guide for everything under Feng Shui.

This book consists of all the information available regarding feng shui. The chapters in the book have been laid out in a progressive manner and aim to serve as a guide for inculcating feng shui in your life to obtain positive results.

The book also includes a brief history of feng shui, the concepts that brought together the feng shui, and how you can utilize the elements of life for your benefit. There are also chapters that deal with specific health benefits of feng shui like stress relief. The book will also help you get started with feng shui and use the resources around you in the best way possible.

Thank you once again for purchasing this book as you step into embracing feng shui and live a better, more peaceful life.

Chapter 1
Feng Shui-What and Why?

What is Feng Shui?

Feng shui is a conventional art of living, which was designed on Chinese philosophy, which has not only a spiritual but also a cultural importance. In simple terms, feng shui can be described as a concept of living in harmony with the surroundings around us. The immediate surroundings were forged into five natural elements of the world that are utilized in feng shui practices. The principles of feng shui are extremely ancient and date back to 4000 BC. Feng shui is still followed by active populations of all cultures worldwide. Most doctors recommend it, as it is associated with various psychological benefits like the relaxation of the mind.

Veronica Fujii

Feng shui commonly referred to as Kanyu, involves designing a home and its contents in a way that there exists a balance between the home and the immediate surroundings. As the tradition has been passed down for generations, cultural and social issues were affected by the natural, cosmological, and metaphysical factors. The West Han dynasty in China introduced the concept of feng shui around the third century to the world based upon the belief that the earth as a living entity has life and energy. The energy of the earth possessed by a location or an object deep within known as 'chi' is influenced by its geography and the surrounding environment. Therefore, a site, which possesses positive energy levels, provides positive energy for those who live on it whereas a site with negative energy harms people who live on it.

Feng shui is is taken into full consideration in Chinese architecture, which included designing Chinese cities around concentric rectangles, which were then surrounded by walls, gardens, valleys, lakes, and other flora and fauna. The rich and poor alike practiced this, and their homes were constructed in a manner, which had a positive effect on the relationships, which exist among individual members of the family. According to the theory of feng shui, the left side of the house is a center for the male energy force known as Yang, which is linked to the energy of heaven. On the other hand, the right side is a center of the female energy force known as Yin, which is linked to the energy forces of the earth. feng shui aims to create a balance with Yin and Yang, which holds the prosperity of your apartment.

Principles of Feng Shui

Feng shui isn't just about repositioning furniture rather it is a lifestyle, which is designed based on concepts of the mind. These concepts require meticulous thinking and have a line of reasoning where they originate. The origin is discussed under the principles of feng shui.

Stability

Feng shui aims to create uniformity and strives to maintain balance. This balance can be achieved in many ways such as through the color arrangement or the arrangement of objects to the numbers associated with your working environment. Your life can achieve a greater sense of stability through the five Earth elements of feng shui and the Bagua. The Bagua is a symmetrical design/pattern, which can be followed for your apartment as it is in complete accordance with the different elements of the earth as per feng shui standards. However, The feng shui standards are unique to each person, but for them to be utilized to their complete potential, they need to be equally complemented.

Sense of Positivity

A sense of positivity can be achieved through feng shui. Most people, who resort to feng shui for help, do so for positive energy. Through positive energy, you can move forward from an irritated and depressed state to one of energetic optimism. Also through an influx of positive energy, all forms of negative energy are eliminated. Once the positive energy of a system is properly utilized, you can ward off the curse of bad luck that has been cast to a location.

Beauty

One of the main concepts of feng shui is to achieve beauty through symmetry according to its principle of symmetry in everything beautiful. This principle strives to achieve beauty and symmetry in everything. Feng shui, is a celebration of the beauty in designing of physical elements that surround us.

Love for Your Environment

Feng shui is environmental friendly and also considers the surroundings around as an active energy source for the construction of places. Feng shui respects the five elements of the earth and makes you more aware of the environment around you. It inspires you to take care of your surroundings and remove any form of negativity that exists with it thereby contributing to your success.

Love for Self

The feng shui principles all have been designed to make you appreciate yourself. This is the most comprehensive way you can attain optimism. When you love yourself, all the negative energy in you will convert itself to positive energy and enhance your productivity. However, love for oneself doesn't imply that your existence is of far more significance than others and doesn't give you a license to indulge in counter-productive activities.

Dreaming

The principles of feng shui are related to multiple entities that are a part of your surroundings. These form a network of several schemes over time. When you dream, the environment around you will provide you different ways, which will let you embrace those dreams, to accomplish your goals. If you dream to become big in life but do not have an adequate environment around you, you will fail.

Feng shui is the art of living, which ensures that you attain a state of stability between your goals in life and the objects that surround you every day.

Why Feng Shui?

Following feng shui in your life will significantly change the way you live when utilized at full potential. Here are the several ways in which your life will change:

- Feng Shui enhances the flow of energies at homes and in workplaces with respect to your environment
- Feng Shui can stabilize the energies of your surroundings for a better scale of life and work

- Feng Shui will bring out the best of the energy of your home or workplace
- Feng Shui utilizes the environment around you as a magnet for opportunities and prosperity
- Feng Shui boosts your good luck improving your personal luck factor
- Feng Shui eliminates the negativity held within a location like geopathic stress.

What is Feng Shui Not?

You may have already begun to wonder where it is that you can begin your journey to achieving feng shui related peace. You worry about where it is the best place for you to arrange your furniture. You may also worry about where there is wealth for you. You could also wonder about how you can activate the different wealth corners too! This section provides you with information that will help you separate the truth from the lies. You will be able to identify the right reasons on why a person follows the feng shui path. There are many misconceptions of the feng shui lifestyle. The main cause of the misconceptions is the Western school of feng shui or the Black Hat Sect Tantric Buddhist feng shui theory.

This theory divides every home into eight segments called the aspirations or the stations of life. These divisions are knowledge, wealth, family, marriage, fame, children, career, and helpful people. This theory uses the front door to identify the orientation of these eight life aspirations or stations. These aspirations match the five elements of the universe – earth, wind, water, metal, and wood. The theory also states that you can use mirrors and crystals to activate these eight life aspirations and stations. They make statements like "A mirror will help to ward off evil spirits," or "Hanging bells inside your door will ring in joy and happiness". These are the most common ideologies of these schools.

It is depressing that these theories and inaccuracies have clouded the ideology of feng shui. These theories have spread far and wide and have made feng shui look like a game that the gullible play. Through this book, you will realize that this is not true. For example, if I had stated that 2 + 2 was 5, would you believe it? Obviously not.

In the same way, feng shui is not a theory that has been built on superstition. It is not a religion and has never been derived from religion. It also does not cure all your problems and is not the elixir of life. It is not even magic! It is not something that has been discovered in the recent times either. You will not lose weight instantly or lose all the wrinkles on your face!

Who Practices Feng Shui?

Here is the truth! Asians are not the only people who practice feng shui. You also do not have to be of Asian descent to practice the theory. You do not have to be a philosopher, an architect, or even a designer to follow the theory. You do not need to meet any criteria to practice feng shui. But there are certain traits that are common to most people who practice feng shui.

- They have an open mind
- They are open to trying alternative methods of therapy if necessary
- They have the belief that every entity in the world is interconnected
- They believe in a Higher Power

- They also believe that there needs to be a harmony in the flow of energies in their body for their well-being
- They believe in Karma, Fate, and Destiny

These people practice feng shui no matter where they are. They cross every barrier that has ever been laid down for the people across the world.

Chapter 2
The Theories of Feng Shui

The 5 Elements of Feng Shui

In Chinese transcript, the words 'feng shui' translate to wind and water respectively. The five elements of feng shui are metal, wood, fire, earth, and water. Feng shui experts state that there should be a sense of equilibrium or harmony among the five elements in your apartment's design. You can grow into an element and increase its coefficients in the formula as per your needs as long as there is a superficial sense of balance.

Metal Elements

If these elements are a part of your furnishing, it promotes money growth or and contribute to your overall financial success. The metal elements are associated with metallic shades of colors like silver, gold, even pieces made from other materials such as stone, marble, or metal. The western corner of your apartment is the ideal spot for metal elements.

Wood Elements

These elements represent loyalty and enhance your creativity and inspirational skills. They are available in various forms for your apartment's designs like the furniture, wood panel walls, or the windowsills. Shades of green can be used instead of the color brown. If your wood element is stationary, the eastern corner of your house or room is preferred.

Fire Elements

The elements of fire are known to assist your efficiency and support passion for getting the job done. It is advisable to position all your fire elements towards the southern corner of the room or house. Fire is extremely strong and is most effective when complimented by the other elements. Hence, care should be taken when a fire element is placed. Red is the color linked most to the fire elements. It is also welcoming and calm to look at. If you do not have a fireplace, you can use candles or lamps as an alternative to represent the fire elements.

Earth Elements

These elements support and offer you a firm foundation for the development of your family relationships. Your apartment could benefit from the addition of earthy colors like the light browns, oranges, and yellows, which will offer a sense of strength to your family. Moreover, you can add clay or ceramic decoration pieces, and walls with portraits of landscapes could add a sense of balance and stability. The center of the room or the house is ideal for the positioning of the earth elements.

Water Elements

Elements of water are represented by fish tanks or miniature fountains and are thought to improve family connections allowing better communication between members of the family. If you do not like fish tanks, you can add an actual water feature or design various features of the house in the colors associated with water like blue and black. When it comes to positioning your mobile water elements, the northern corner of the room or house is recommended.

The Theory of the Universal Energy, Chi

This is a theory that has been taken from the Chinese culture. In their culture, they have stated that the Chi is the energy that is found everywhere in the universe. It is called the spiritual or the universal energy. This energy permeates every entity in the universe! These entities could either be animate or inanimate. The Chi energy is the sole basis for both the Yin and Yang theory and the theory of the five elements in feng shui.

According to the theories in the feng shui, the Chi manifests itself in every possible entity. This means that it could manifest itself in different colors, decors, objects, decors and even the carpets at home! The basic objective of feng shui is to attract all the universal energy or the Chi into your home and thereby into your body. This will ensure a good flow of the energy in your body too!

It is extremely important to ensure that the quality and the quantity of the Chi around you must be alive and vibrant! It is only when this happens that you will have a good flow of energy in your body. The tips given in this book will help you understand how this can be done. You have to remember to remove any blockages that you may have in your house. It is essential that the Chi flow freely. Try to identify the flow of the Chi!

The Yin and Yang Theory

The Yin Yang theory is one ancient teaching taught in most Chinese schools. Most of the traditional Chinese practices of ancient martial arts, medicine, I-Ching, the complete Taoism cosmology, and even feng shui all rise from the dynamics of Yin and Yang.

According to the Ying and Yang theory, every entity in the universe comprises of two opposing yet deeply integrated forces known as the Yin and the Yang. The Yin is regarded as a feminine component whereas the Yang is masculine.

The forces interact and integrate with each other to serve the essence of life. They are independent forces, yet they depend on each for their existence.

As per the colors of feng shui, the Yin, feminine energy is represented by black and the Yang, masculine energy is represented by white. When it comes to the energy levels, Yin is a soft, relaxed, smooth, diffused, calm, passive, and silent force. The true essence of feminine energy is seen in nature as the mystery of the moon, the blackness of rich soil, softness of water, and the deep silence of the night.

On the other side, the Yang force can be represented as a complete opposite to the Yin force. Yang forces are seen with the aggression of racing cars, the fiery heat of the sun, the focused energy of a laser beam, and the solid surface of a mountain rock.

In comparison, Yang is the hot pinch of a summer morning's sun and Yin is the calm and silent mystery of the night.

Feng shui involves the maintenance of a state of balance between forces. For maintaining a balance between Yin and Yang, you should understand the practical application of the

Yin Yang theory on a simple level in order to benefit from the positive energies.

Yin

Ying, a passive energy, is the feng shui force of relaxation that you can implement in rooms where you need to be calm and relaxed like your bedroom or your bathroom. Yin can be represented by calm colors, soothing art, portraits of babies, and soft music.

Yang

Yang, an active energy is the feng shui force linked to strong colors, bright lights, vibrant sounds, loud music indicating an uprising force. Yang energy should be well distributed all over your home or workplace, even in your kitchen, and at parties you host.

Your home cannot isolate the Yin and Yang forces hence you will have to find stability between both the energies. A good example of a home that uses feng shui for balance will project a homogenous rhythm between both active and passive energies. In today's fast-paced world, unknowingly you create an imbalance of feng shui energies. The world is extremely active, feisty, busy, and full of Yang forces. In this process, we lose out on the Yin forces. A balance between the Yin Yang forces has to be reestablished.

Yin Energy in Your Home

Your bedroom should be constructed around Yin energy in order to heal you. Gradually, you will have to let go of the cluttering Yang elements in the bedroom like your TV or your office machinery.

But one shouldn't go overboard with the Yang elimination. A balance has to be maintained while the Yin energy serves as the predominant energy in your bedroom for the relaxation and elimination of your toxins. You will need the presence of Yang elements such as red candles and bright colors to contrast the Yin. This applies for your bathroom in a similar fashion.

Yang Energy in Your Home

On the other hand, rooms like your living room, your family room, your study table, and your kitchen are hotspots for accepting the benefits of Fen Shui forces and Yang energy. Integrate vibrant colors, upbeat music, with a variety of feng shui decor accessories that provide the environment around with positive uprising energy.

Balancing Yin and Yang

If you feel an energy imbalance in your home, it is most probably under the influence of unstable Yin Yang. However, balancing Yin and Yang forces isn't a cumbersome process.

To balance Yin or the relaxing energy, introduce calming forces like earth elements. To balance Yang, the active energy, inculcate bright colors with upbeat music to restore balance.

Attaining a state of peace between Yin and Yang forces in your feng shui home will bring out the positive forces, which are needed to live a healthy and prosperous life.

Veronica Fujii

Chapter 3
Getting Started with Feng Shui

Feng shui is a core component of ancient Chinese art and science. It bridges the energy gap between you and your environment through a beneficial relationship. It believes in the concept that nature is an active host of energy. To embrace feng shui, you must indulge in the act of arranging objects around your home or workplace in a symmetrical fashion to attract positive energy.

Feng shui does not require building a harmonious home with expensive and exquisite tools. It is rather all about sticking to the basic aspects in an attempt to attract the right energies into your apartment.

Feng Shui Basics For Your Home

Embracing feng shui in your house's layout does not have to be that complicated. There are several ways through which you can integrate feng shui into your house and absorb the positive energy that emerges. There are certain basic feng shui practices that pack high levels of positive energy know as Chi and can be easily applied for your house.

Feng Shui, Light, Air

To have your apartment as a positive energy source, it needs to be provided with good quality air as well as adequate lighting. According to the feng shui, chi, the positive energy flows with aid from the air and natural light. Accordingly, these two core elements are to be regulated at all times to ensure the flow of good chi in the house. Once you open windows and allow the natural air and light in, it will allow proper recycling of energies in the house. If the air around your locality isn't healthy and pure, you can also plant purifying saplings or install an air purifier at home to ensure a steady flow of non-toxic air. Allow as much as natural light into your house as you can to keep your house bright and not dull.

Decluttering

Decluttering is an important practice of embracing feng shui. Clutter forms a barrier and doesn't allow the flow of chi across your house. This affects the health of the people who live in the house as the overall energy levels are low which affects the quality of life. Too much of your junk cannot only attract high levels of negative energy but also could contribute in the eradication of the positive energy in your life. Get rid of the clutter development at your house and allow an influx of positivity. As you clean up the environment around you, you are providing yourself and your home better surroundings to live in.

Feng Shui Birth Element

Birth elements correspond to the year you were born and establishes a better sense of understanding for the utilization of feng shui. There is a certain element that corresponds to your birth year. Knowledge of the element can assist you in establishing better relationships and in optimizing your home with optimistic and powerful unharnessed energy. There are also several lucky stones that can help increase the positivity in the room. If you place a particular stone like the hematite in the room, then it can affect the aura of the room. You need to find out what stone will benefit you and instead of picking random ones as the wrong stone can affect the room in a negative way.

Know Your Kua Number

As per the principles of feng shui, a kua number depicts the strength of a person's energy requirements. It gives information regarding your energy needs. When it comes to kua numbers, people belong to one of two energy groups, which are referred to as the East or the West. For the East group, the kua numbers are given by 1, 3, 4 or 9. On the other hand, for those on the West group, the kua numbers are 2, 6, 7 or 8. Your kua number's characteristics serve to give you specific guidelines related to the directions and orientation of structures such as your apartment or the positioning of objects to ensure a steady and consistent flow of chi in the apartment.

As you apply these feng shui basics for your home, you will experience positive results and optimism, all through the uninterrupted positive air that flows through your home

Home Décor with Feng Shui

Feng shui is all about attaining a state of stability between various elements of your surroundings, which in turn brings positive energy and good fortune. The practice of feng shui is localized to your own house and its immediate surroundings. Apart from the basic feng shui integrations, there are also areas of home decoration that you should follow for greater balance between the elements. Decorating your home with feng shui is one step further when compared to the necessities.

Layout

When you begin, draw a layout of your entire apartment, which will help you with the orientations and directions. While drawing a layout, ensure that you are marking the north points. Use the Bagua map and map out all the elements. This will be especially beneficial during the initial stages of the decorating, as you will have the chance to incorporate feng shui without having to get rid of something that already exists.

Work on the Door

When you design your apartment's layout, avoid lining the front and back door in a straight path. As per the principles of feng shui, if a straight path were followed from the entry to the exit, the energy would pass through and wouldn't be beneficial. If your home has this kind of arrangement, add an angled obstruction or an object to add a curve to the path, allowing a sideward-flow of energy.

Let There Be Light

The more natural light your apartment receives, the more energy flow it experiences. If there is no natural light coming in, then you can make use of tube lights that will introduce a light that is as bright as sunlight. If you have a roof on top, then consider cutting away two or three small holes through the ceiling and placing Malaysian glass roof tiles to allow some natural light to filter in. As décor, you can add green plants where there is sufficient light available. Green in feng shui is a color of happiness as it is an earth element. Apart from plants, your home could have wind chimes, mirrors, and portraits painted with bright colors to experience more energy flow. Hang the wind chimes wherever there is a steady supply of wind. The constant chimes will help you feel relaxed, and all your stress will be driven away.

Water Elements

A burst of water refreshes Chi. Water elements, such as a miniature water fountain, could bring good fortune for your family. The fountain should be positioned in the center of the apartment. Additionally, you can add a fish tank with some goldfish, which is a positive sign as it encourages wealth. The fish tank, however, will require your care and attention in ensuring that there is no stagnation. You can also add in some freshwater plants to the fish tank to incorporate the element of earth but make sure that these plants are suitable for aquariums so that they won't harm your fish or die out themselves.

The Element of Red

Red as a color is visual appealing. In feng shui, red is a significant color as it marks passion and celebrations. You can utilize the color for your bedrooms or the living room. However, too much red is linked to cases of restlessness, overstimulation and anger issues. Red is ideal for the detailing of your house accessories and decorations. So try having a few red drapes in your house to add in some color as well as to up the level of excitement. Don't be afraid to paint any one wall red and leave the rest plain. This is a visual trick that is generously used in home decoration.

The South Points

As you mark the north points of the apartment, you can pay more attention to the south. The south area is an important area for optimizing the flow of chi as it helps in the development of satisfying relationships. This area should be free from clutter and be filled with objects that are available in pairs such as candles or dolls.

The Dining Room

For your dining area, your decorating should involve circular items as they bring heavenly blessings. The number of chairs at the dining table should be an even number as it marks balance. Minimal decoration for this area promotes healthier eating, as there will be no distractions. If you have a crockery cabinet, then make sure that it is made of wood. An all-glass structure might not be a good choice. Also, maintain a neat cabinet and don't simply throw all your crockery inside it. Arrange it in such a way that all the bowls are stacked inside each other and all the spoons are placed inside the bowls. Having proper lighting inside the cabinet can improve the flow of energy.

Exposed Beams

Watch out for any exposed beams around the house. If there are any, cover them up because, in feng shui principles, they create an opposing energy flow that forces the chi flow to the bottom. This can have a negative effect on your health and fortune. You can either cover it or remove everything from underneath it.

Bedroom

When it comes to the bedroom, your arrangement shouldn't involve placing a mirror directly opposite to the bed as it is known to cause relationship problems, often involving a third party.

Placing some fresh plants in the bedroom is a great idea as it will completely purify the air inside your room and also add in a dash of color.

Your home can achieve peace and prosperity once it has been completely decorated and revamped as per the principle of feng shui. It is always advised to start with the basics of feng shui for your home and then move ahead to the décor part.

The next chapters deal with the tips you can use to feng shui your house up!

Chapter 4
Feng Shui Auspicious Symbols and Tokens

There are several symbols and tokens that are considered to be lucky and would attract good luck or good feng shui. Some of them are given below:

Buddha

Buddha idols are extremely popular in the use of Feng Shui because they are considered to be very lucky. When these idols are placed in the appropriate locations, they bring good luck. They also allow positive energy to flow freely, bringing balance to the house. Buddha idols are not bought but are gifted, as one can't buy their own happiness. They come in various shapes and sizes. They also come in several colors.

Lucky Coins

You often see yellow coins, which are small and have a square hole in the middle; these are called the lucky coins of feng shui. They are usually tied with red ribbons or red thread and hung from the ceilings or kept on tablets. For this purpose, two or more coins are used. These coins are believed to increase the financial status of a person. They also absorb the negative energy in the room. It is best to tie the number of coins based on your lucky number. These coins are easily found online or in Chinese stores.

Totems

Totems are influential items that can impact a particular corner of a room or an office. They are often golden colored and come in different shapes. They commonly take animal forms or bird shapes or even golden spheres. They can be placed in various corners of the house to allow positive energy flow. Again, these can be found online or bought from Chinese stores.

Crystals

Crystals are auspicious across several cultures. They are often known to be able to cleanse areas. Therefore, Chinese culture uses crystals to purify and absorb all the bad energy in the area that they are placed. You can also use colored stones along with the crystals to complement them. The colored stones can depend on the colors used in feng shui based on the direction of the room.

Aquariums

Aquariums are a decorative way to incorporate the water element into your home. It is best to place aquariums in the corner of the room where the element of water is strongest to maximize the benefits of this element. Alternatively, fountains can also be used.

Plants

Plants are considered to be very holy in the Chinese culture. They bring good luck and prosperity as they represent the element of wood. You can choose appropriate plants based on what you are looking for. For instance, plants like the Areca palm (*Chrysalidocarpus lutescens*) can solve problems in family life and relationships, while bamboo and cacti can bring harmony and peace. There are many sites online that list what benefits certain plants can offer in your home.

As human beings, we are always trying to define things. We try to place things in a way to give us a sense of control and order. This is not a recent development. Man's execution and showcasing of superiority and control has around since the dawn of civilization. Originally we were nature worshippers called pantheists and since the times of old we have been seeing positive energy and negative energy and attributing those energies to symbols and depictions to create meaning. We try to identify with positive aura and automatically collect tokens that bring us positive aura and minimize those items and tokens that give us negative aura. We observe certain things that hold meaning for us and throw light on how its existence impacts us. We observe and contemplate on these symbols, and there are several forms of studies for these symbols.

These studies show how these symbols and tokens enable us to weave our own path. The energy flow of life, its dynamics, and mechanisms are touched upon by the Wu Xing. Wu Xing is a theory that talks about how symbols have power; it classifies these symbols or tokens into five categories based on their energy flow, their movements, and their agents that are representatives of life. Since ancient civilizations worshiped nature, and feng shui is an ancient Chinese practice, the Chinese have attributed that anything that has been created will only confer to these five elements. Water, wood, fire, metal, and earth are the five elements that are classified according to the Wu Xing principle.

Listed below are just a few of the many symbols that are attributed to the Feng Shui principle Wu Xing. These tokens are ones that can have an impact on a person's life. There are several types of symbols from fruit symbols, flower symbols, seasons, numbers, and even bird symbols.

Fruit Symbols

Feng shui has been adopted from nature, and they are mostly nature centric practices. For instance, when a seed is turned into a fruit, the energy used for this process to take place is taken into account in feng shui. Feng shui principles state that the energy that was used in the process of development is stored within the fruit, and this energy is present throughout the life span of the fruit. This energy can help harness luck, observe negative energy, and emit positive energy. Some fruits are very popular among the Chinese. These are usually fruits that are traditionally grown in China. Fruits like pomegranates, pineapples, peaches, grapes, apples, and oranges are considered good sources of positive energy. These fruits emit positive energy forces, and each symbolizes a particular aspect. These fruits are some of the most popular fruits that are used in the ancient art of feng shui and are extensively described in vast details about their properties in ancient documents, transcripts, and inscriptions. They are considered to be supreme symbols of prosperity, good health, wealth, longevity, fertility, etc.

The fruits are often symbolized and classified by their colors, numbers, texture, and the aspects they resemble in the art of feng shui. Often these fruits were not native to many regions as China was a rice cultivating, agriculture economy. As these fruits were expensive, despite being native to China, many people could not afford these fruits. Therefore, they were unable to benefit from the luck these fruits offered. It is important to display fresh fruit, however, with busy schedules and lives it is almost impossible to keep track of the fresh fruits and this why feng shui is also flexible. People found that it is possible to harness this luck with pictures and paintings of these fruits when the fruits themselves are unattainable. These pieces of art form a part of the decor and are considered good feng shui. They can also be hung as charms and wall hangings. In fact, certain compounds like crystal, when shaped into certain fruits, can emit positive energy. This is also applicable to brass items that can be kept around the house as a part of home furnishings to promote good luck. Amulets, trinkets, charms, and other small items with fruit pictures or inscriptions in them can also promote good luck.

Listed below are just some of the symbols that have been used since ancient times for the practices of feng shui in China. It includes the fruits in terms of their applications, meaning, attributes, and symbolism.

Grapes:

Grapes are usually fruits that come in a bunch. As they are not found alone on a vine, grapes depict abundance and quantity. It represents plenty. The interesting point here is that grapes have been associated with abundance and quantity across several nations like Greece, Rome, India, and so on. In the art of feng shui, grapes depict abundance too, but they are attributed towards abundant success. It is associated with material wealth that has been a byproduct due to a person's success. Grapes also are tokens of fertility. The energy in grapes converts the bad luck that is present around you into good luck. It is best to keep grapes in fruit bowls in the house. Alternatively, you can also have pictures and paintings of grapes that will bring you good luck.

Peach:

Ancient scriptures and inscriptions that throw light on the practices and symbols of feng shui associates peaches with heaven. The Chinese have attributed that peach is a fruit that has come to earth from heaven and that it is the fruit of the immortal gods and goddesses since ancient times. Peaches, therefore, are attributed to longevity and are symbols of immortality. They are linked to good health, wealth and prosperity, and long life. Peaches aren't just limited to symbolizing long life through good health; they also symbolize harmony in marriage and love. Chinese sayings state that peach is a symbol of good life, good health, and good marriage. Thus, it is said that this regal fruit is associated with plenty of luck.

Pineapple:

Pineapples are fruit that are common tokens for the coming of good fortune and good luck. Basically, as per the Chinese, it is attributed towards good luck that is going to come soon. Pineapples are symbols of good fortune, abundant wealth, and prosperity. It is for this reason that most Chinese houses have a pineapple. Pineapples are usually kept in the living room to ward off bad energy and bad luck. Paintings of pineapples are also kept as a part of the home furnishings.

Apple:

The art of feng shui associates apples with harmony and health. Apples have always denoted good health, good luck, and peace. The rich, vibrant red of the apple is one of the lucky colors in feng shui, and it is, for this reason, that Chinese robes and decors have a hint of red in them. The red apples are considered very auspicious and are used for functions. The Chinese word for apple closely resembles the Chinese word for peace and hence apples are also associated with good harmony. Since apples come in different colors, they denote different things based on their color. The red apple was native to China and is, therefore, more traditional. However, thanks to differences in soil, science, technology, and the breaking of cultural barriers, the production of different varieties of apple has become possible.

Pomegranate:

The ancient practice of feng shui associates the delicious seeds of a pomegranate to that of fertility. Pomegranate as per the ancient Chinese texts is attributed to fertility and happiness. This particular fruit brings in good luck and increases the happiness of the family. It also is considered to make pregnant mothers have a smooth motherhood. Feng shui practices aim at having pomegranates in fruit baskets in the house. Alternatively, a picture or a painting of the fruit is also symbolic of good luck and young newlyweds often keep these pictures to conceive children. They should also keep art forms of pomegranates as a part of their house decor for keeping positive energy in the house and attracting good luck.

Orange:

The practical uses of this citrus fruit are plenty. Its flavors are commonly used to cleanse and purify things. Its fresh flavor is extensively used in cooking and several body deodorants, lotions, and creams because of its fresh, clean properties and thus it is no surprise that in feng shui, this particular fruit is associated with cleansing or refreshing odor and purification. This fruit has a yang quality because its orange color cleanses and purifies. It also eradicates bad luck. Oranges are usually bought in a group of nine; this is because nine oranges are said to provide good luck when kept in the living room or the kitchen.

Flower Symbols:

Flowers are extensively used all over the world. Since ancient times flowers have been related to grace, poise, delicateness, sensuality, and beauty. In feng shui flowers are used to evoke positive feelings. Usually, it is fresh flowers that are kept for homes. Fresh flowers are full of life and energy. Thus, they also emit positive energy through their pleasant fragrance. Silk flowers or paintings of flowers and wall decorations that have prints of flowers in them are also used as substitutes to fresh flowers in feng shui.

Flowers are attributed to blessings, good harmony, and balance of life, peace, serenity, and good luck. Flowers have the properties of chi, which is the flow of positive energy into houses

Like every other symbol in feng shui, flowers are classified based on their quantity, colors, and the symbols that they represent. Charms, bracelets, artifacts, and decorative items that have prints of flowers are considered good feng shui. Listed below are a bunch of famous flower symbols that are extensively used in the application of Feng Shui:

Cherry Blossoms:

Cherry blossoms are beautiful young flowers that are small and delicate. Just like the flowers, they depict youthfulness, innocence, and freshness. They are used as blessings during weddings and newlyweds often have a bunch of them to represent young love and romance. They also eradicate problematic marriages and are also symbolic to good health.

Chrysanthemum:

Chrysanthemums are flowers that are often attributed to the balance of life. It also represents harmony and peace. The strong yang energy present in these flowers are those that attract good vibes into your home.

Lotus:

Lotus flowers depict strength and purity. This is because lotuses are grown in marshy lands, and they blossom untouched by the dirt found in the marshy land. Thus they symbolize strength, purity, and harmony. Lotuses are also used for several purposes; its roots are used as vegetables and are also used for medicinal purposes. Thus, they not only symbolize purity but also are harbingers of good health and longevity.

Narcissus:

Narcissus are flowers that are symmetrical and structured. It is because of these physical aspects of this flower that it is often associated with organization, positive energy, career growth, and success. They are also symbols of abilities and talents. They are used and kept in houses where there are problems with one's career. They are also representations of the rewards or the fruit that is begotten out of hard and sincere work. Though yellow and white narcissus are present, white is more popular.

Orchids:

Orchids in the art of feng shui are interpreted as symbols for fertility. They also represent quantity, abundance, purity, beauty, and spirituality. Orchids are not just used by the Chinese; in fact, even Western countries affix some denotations to orchids usually along the same lines.

Peony:

The peony is considered to be the national flower of China. These flowers have a mild amazing scent, which is used in perfumes and body lotions. The pleasant fragrance of peonies is related to sensuality. Peony symbolizes love, romance, and harmony. Thus, it is not surprising that peonies are found as decorations at weddings and other romantic endeavors. Pink peonies are also representative of beauty.

Bird Symbols:

In feng shui, most of the living aspects consist of energy and this energy can be both positive as well as negative. In feng shui, it is advisable to choose a bird that represents who you are. You must also feel connected to that bird.

Birds are considered to be the passing of difficulties; these symbols represent new beginnings and new chances for a person. They are also attributed to good luck, harmony, commitment, love, and abundance.

Like all the aspects of feng shui, different birds symbolize different things. These differences arise based on the number of birds, their colors, and the symbolism that each bird upholds. Birds can't usually be kept at home, and it is for this purpose that bird symbols are usually used in charms and home decors to promote good feng shui. Listed below are some of the bird symbols that are commonly used in the art of feng shui.

Cranes:

Cranes are extremely popular in Chinese usage. They are the second most popular bird that is used for the applications of feng shui. Crane patterns are used in fabrics as prints, embroidered items, and patchwork. They are also used in decorative pieces, sculptures, art, paintings, crystal pieces, or even fabric that is used in households. Due to the long life span of this particular bird, it represents qualities like longevity. In Chinese culture, it is believed that the souls of those who have passed away are carried to heaven by these birds and hence it is considered a noble bird. These birds are also attributed to harmony, peace, and serenity.

Phoenix:

The phoenix is one of the most popular birds in the Chinese culture. These birds are mythical creatures and their prints are used in fabrics, decoration items, and crockery. It is often associated with the dragon, and the combination of the phoenix and dragon creates balance and harmony. This is because, in feng shui, dragons denote a happy married life. A phoenix is comprised of the yang symbol, and the dragon symbolizes the yin symbol. When the two forces of yin and yang are combined, they give birth to harmony and balance. The Phoenix is considered a holy bird in Chinese cultures; this is because it is believed that this celestial bird guards the entrances of houses. It is also associated with positive energy because of the element it possesses. Phoenix are birds of fire and hence their element is fire. This is attributed to the energy related to transformation, great strength, courage, and resilience.

Mandarin Ducks:

In the Chinese culture, Mandarin ducks are considered to be lovebirds. Hence, they are used in the applications of feng shui. Mandarin ducks represent affection, devotion, respect, and loyalty, which are keys to any good relationships. These birds are typically used to sort issues and resolve conflict among couples, especially in the romantic aspect. Mandarin ducks are often found only in pairs, and it is for this reason that their depictions are also the same way. Since these ducks only come in pairs, they represent romance, love, and relationships. They are usually painted on the walls of bedrooms or are used as decorative pieces in bedrooms. This is because the bedroom signifies the blending of two souls into one.

Peacock:

Peacocks are beautiful multicolored and majestic birds, and it is because of these aspects that they are considered to be incarnations of phoenixes. The Chinese believe that peacocks are the manifestation of the Phoenix on earth. Their stunning iridescent bodies are a representation of beauty. They are famous for the several colors that their bodies possess. The feathers that are present are believed to be the thousand eyes of the bird and these eyes promote prestige, fame, and luck as per the practices of feng shui. Peacocks are also attributed to physical beauty, attraction, romance, love, and marriage. The feathers of peacocks are used to attract a partner for a long and peaceful marriage.

Rooster:

Roosters in Chinese culture are symbols of a person's progress in his or her career. The Chinese word for rooster is also the word for officials. Roosters are also harbingers of peace and good luck. It is believed that the cry of the roosters before the sunrise wards off the darkness and the spirits and the unholy omens that are associated with darkness. Roosters are overbearing in terms of quality. According to the applications of feng shui, a person should know the direction that is lucky for him or her and place the rooster in that direction.

Doves:

Doves are usually white in color, and the color white is often associated with peace, serenity, and harmony. In fact, across most cultures and countries doves represent peace and harmony. They are also symbols of romance and hence in feng shui these birds are also used to resolve conflict and ensure a peaceful and harmonious balance between couples. In ancient Chinese legends and texts, doves were used to maintain peace in the palace. This is because, doves produce a very calming sound, and this has a positive effect on a person's mind.

Magpie:

Magpies are beautiful little birds. In Chinese cultures, it is believed that magpies are holy signs and spotting a magpie could mean a revolutionary change in the positive direction for the person seeing it. It is attributed to bringing new opportunities and new changes. This is not limited to just a person's career; it also includes romance, love, family relationships, friendships, and any and all other aspects. They are attributed towards success, opportunities, new beginnings, chances, joy, and celebration. They also are lucky for those people who are searching for a new home. It is believed that having depictions or charms of these birds can imply that the search is over and that the person will go into a new home and lead a happy, peaceful life. They also represent happy marriage, good households, and joyous children. It is believed that having depictions of this bird can clear any hurdles that a person is facing.

Color Symbols:

Colors too play an important role in feng shui. But it isn't just the mere colors that play an important role; the directions in which certain objects are kept are also taken into consideration. Some directions and colors are harmonious as opposed to others.

In the North Direction:

In feng shui, it is believed that northern areas or the northern zone of the place are the directions that will increase the career opportunities and financial standards of the person. It is important to know that there exist both positive as well as negative colors. Listed below are few of the colors that go hand in hand with the north direction.

Colors That Give Negative Results:

Like stated before, some colors have a positive impact, and some have a negative impact in terms of direction. Those areas or rooms that are situated on the northern side, the colors that have a negative impact are earth tones and shades such as pink, brown, or yellow. Other colors such as skin or taupe colors as well as green are also considered negative. These colors are those that represent wood.

Now the important thing to note is, if you do happen to have a kitchen or a toilet on the northern side of the house then wood colors will actually have a positive effect. This is because it will absorb the negative energy that is present in the dirty water from the kitchen and toilet. These colors, when used in toilets and kitchen, will help to increase your luck in the career-sphere. Earthen tones can also be used, but these colors are very aggressive in nature and hence have a very strong impact. Thus, it is better to avoid them.

Rooms such as the living room, when placed in the northern direction of the house should be painted in colors like blue. This is because the shades of blue are calming, and it represents serenity and tranquility. Blue is also a color that helps to reduce appetite. For instance, eating from a blue plate is generally said to reduce your appetite. However, take care not to use the blue shades everywhere because it can cause depression. They can also cause illness, tiredness, and so on. So the key is to maintain balance, paint in a slightly bright shades of blue and don't overdo the blue paint in your house.

Colors That Give Positive Results:

Those areas in the house or work spot that are situated on the northern side of the entire house or office that have a good feng shui are colors such as silver, gray, white, and gold. If you notice, these colors are usually metallic colors. Water-based colors such as blue and black are also good.

In the South Direction:

In Chinese culture, it is believed that the rooms or work spot that belongs to the southern side of the house or office has an impact on the social status, name, and fame of the family.

Colors That Give Negative Results:

Colors that result in adverse effects when painted on the southern side are aquatic colors like blue and black. Colors like yellow or skin tones and other colors that represent the earth also have a negative effect.

Colors That Give Positive Results:

Colors that have a positive impact on the person are bright and vibrant colors such as reds, greens, and other wooden tones. These colors are shades that represent the elements of fire and wood.

If you need the attention, popularity, and you want to appear superior or of some status to your peers and colleagues you will need to take care of the southern parts of your place. If you have bathrooms and kitchens on the southern side of the house, it is a good idea to paint these rooms in earthen tones of yellow or taupe. This will eradicate the negative effects of the room. It is important to balance everything; this will result in the reduction of negative attention. This can be in the form of gossip or lack of recognition in the society, or any such reason that will bring the family name down.

If the living room is in the southern part of the house, it is advisable to paint this room a good shade of red. This promotes happiness as the color red is attributed to being a very auspicious color according to the Chinese. Red is also a color that can increase your appetite. This is the reason hotels, especially Chinese hotels, are painted in shades of red. This color also acts as a stimulant and revives various parts of the brain.

It is important to use the right shade of red, to avoid too much of gaudiness or garishness. Also, if you use too much red, it can have a very negative impact. Red is also associated with negative emotions such as anger, rage, and impatience. The brain can get stimulated to channel these emotions if there is too much red in the room. Thus, balance is the key. It is important to keep the ratio as 1:10. It is advisable to use other colors that are wood colors to balance excessive red, like green, brown and so on. This will create harmony and bring balance.

In the East and Southeast Directions:

This direction is important as it has an impact on wealth and assets. The east and southeast directions of the house are the corners for property, wealth, and investments. Using colors representative of the water and wood elements are good and will have a positive impact. The eastern direction of the houses usually represents health. Wood colors like browns and greens have a positive effect because they keep the mind calm and happy and have a good impact on the health.

Colors That Give Negative Results:

Colors that represent the element of fire such as shades of red or orange and colors that symbolize metal such as gray, silver, and gold can have a negative effect on the person. This is particularly true if the room facing the eastward direction is painted in these shades.

Colors That Give Positive Results:

Colors that represent the element of wood, such as brown tones or green shades are good for these directions. Also, colors such as black and blue that represent water have a positive impact on the house. It is advisable to paint the kitchens and washrooms that are facing these directions in shades of red, orange, or any other shade that represents the element of fire. Generally, it is better to not construct a toilet or a kitchen on these sides of the house. They are known to have a bad effect on the health as this direction represents health. They also have a bad impact on the investments, properties and other assets that the household possesses.

Green is a color that gives out positive vibes. It keeps one in good spirits and good health. It also keeps them fit and healthy. Alternately, colors like gold, gray, and silver can also be used. Green is a better color as it represents nature and derives the energy from nature. Hence, green is also a very auspicious color in feng shui for this direction. It has a calming impact on the mind and body. It is best to use various shades of green and not stick to one particular tone. You can also use it with other colors especially water-like colors of blue and black.

In West and Northwest Directions:

For the rooms that are situated in these directions, it is best to paint in the colors that represent metals like silver, white, and gold and the earth tones such as yellow and shades of skin colors. The West and Northwest directions are the ones that impact progeny. This area is associated with the behavior and luck of the child. It also impacts conceiving the child. In Chinese culture, it is believed that this area brings celestial luck. It also impacts travel.

Colors That Bring in Negative Energy:

It is best to avoid colors that represent the element of fire. Some examples of these are shades of red or orange; this is because it can stimulate the brain cells into channeling emotions of rage and anger. Also, it is advisable to avoid colors that are opposite as well like blue and black which are colors of the water element because it can represent fatigue and illness.

Colors That Bring in Positive Energy:

It is best to use the colors that represent the nature of land such as pink, yellow, and brown. You can also paint the rooms in this direction in metallic shades of gold, white, and silver. This will have a positive effect.

Kitchens or bathrooms that are located in this region should be painted in colors that represent the water element like blue and black. This will absorb the negative energy present. It is also best to avoid building a lavatory or a kitchen in these directions as it can impact a pregnant woman.

If there are living rooms present in this direction, it is ideal to paint them metallic colors like silver, gray or gold. This will create warmth and keep the family positive. It is also important to not use these shades in excess as they can also be dull colors and make a person dull.

When using these colors, it is a good idea to use patterns or various shades to prevent monotony. Alternatively you can use textures and add colorful materials to embellish these dull colors. This will bring liveliness. You can also pair dull colors with slightly more vibrant tones like yellow and so on. This will balance the energy around and create peace and harmony. You can also use colors such as pink, brown, and skin tones. You can also use combinations of these colors on your decorative items. The walls can be gray, your furniture can be a light taupe color and the decor can be yellow and so on.

In Northeast and Southwest Directions:

The northeast and southwest directions are considered to be important especially for those looking for love. These directions have an impact on the way a person's romantic love or marriage life is. Therefore, problems or wrong colors in these places can result in adverse effects. Positive colors that go with these directions have a good impact on the couple or family life and can lead to happiness.

Colors that symbolize the element of fire such as orange or red are colors that are suitable for the southwest direction. It is also advisable to use colors that represent the element of earth like that of green or brown. This will help in education and progress in academics. Good colors that support these directions have an excellent impact. It is believed that right colors can make people in the house make good decisions and enable right choices. They also see an improvement in their family life. Students and children who are studying will have a bright future and they will shine in academic endeavors.

Colors That Have Negative Impacts:

Colors that represent the element of wood such as browns and other wooden tones like yellow, as well as shades that are metallic in nature such as gold, white, or gray are not suitable for the house as they will have a negative impact on the place as well as the people of the house.

Colors That Have Positive Impacts:

Earth tones and colors that represent the element of fire like yellow, orange, and red will have a positive impact on the house and the people in the house.

Bathrooms and kitchens that are placed in these areas should be painted in colors like gray, silver, and other metallic shades. These will reduce the bad effects and absorb the negative energy.

Now it is important to note that the colors that represent nature of wood can also be used but they have a tendency to be very overpowering and can impact the overall effect. Thus it is best to use these tones in moderation and combine them with shades of metal to neutralize and bring balance to the entire room.

Living rooms in these directions should be painted in colors that represent the element of earth such as yellows and pinks can be used. It is advisable to use pink in the living room as it is said to have a calming effect. Alternatively you can use the color yellow, which is vibrant and bright. This will have a positive effect, it will keep the energy balanced, and it will lead to a cheerful and a happy life. This will also increase the concentration and memory levels of the students living in this place and hence have a good effect on their education or profession.

Now you will have noticed that everything is interwoven. One particular element or color is related to a particular direction of the house. This is because of the principles of nature where a balance is key for harmony and peace. Therefore, it is ideal to paint or decorate your house according to the color scheme that gives balance.

Numbers and Seasons Symbols:

Like stated in the previous section, everything is connected and interwoven. Thus, elements and seasons and numbers also have an impact. We shall take a look at these in this section.

The element for southern, southeast, and eastern corners is wood, and thus the colors like browns and greens are appropriate. Thus, it is ideal to have a garden in this direction or have potted plants.

The element for the south, southwest, and the northeast corners is fire, and so the colors such as oranges and shades of reds should be used. It is smart to keep a fireplace in this area of the house.

The element of earth is the element thought of for the center, southwest and northeast. It is better to use earthen shades such as beige, yellow, and so on to decorate these areas. It is best to use decorative items like posters and photographs for this portion of the house.

The element of metal is the element that relates with the west, north, and northwest. Thus metallic shades like silver, white, and gray can be used in these places. You can use metallic sculptures and metal decorative items in these areas.

The element for the north, southeast, and east is water, and so the colors that are represented by these elements are shades of blues and blacks. It is ideal to keep water fountains or aquariums in these locations.

Each area of the house will also be associated with a particular season. The seasons are given as below:

All the seasons are focused on the center of the house. The beginning of the summer is represented in the south; while the late summer or the ending of the summer is represented for the southwest. The onset of spring is represented in the east and the season of spring is represented in southeast. West is associated with early fall and northwest is for late fall. North is represented by early winter and northeast is represented by late winter.

Now this information is quite useful for decorative items. The season associated with these directions can be represented through pictures, showpieces, decorative items, and prints and so on.

Seasons, elements, directions and finally, numbers. Numbers, too have a particular representation in feng shui for all the directions. Some numbers are considered quite lucky for certain areas. Let's take a look at what these numbers are. The lucky numbers for each direction are as follows:

- 5 is the lucky number for the center of the house.

- 9 is the lucky number for the south direction.

- 4 is the lucky number for the southeast direction.

- 2 is the lucky number for the southwest direction.

- 1 is the lucky number for the north direction.

- 6 is the lucky number for the northwest direction.

- 8 is the lucky number for the northeast direction.

- 3 is the lucky number for the east direction.

Lucky numbers are not just limited to rooms; they also are lucky for people. Lucky numbers for a particular person is called a Kua number. The number is calculated using your date of birth and gender. The calculation for the Kua number is given below.

For females:

· Add the last two numbers of your birth year. You will now get one single number.

· Add this number to the number 5. If the result is a two-digit number, add the digits to get a single number.

· The final result will be your Kua number.

For males:

· Add the last two numbers of your birth year. You will now get one single number.

· Deduct that number from number 10.

· The difference is your Kua number.

Veronica Fujii

Chapter 5
Feng Shui Tips for Your Home

- Marble is known to attract geopathic stress. Hence, a marble table in the house is not good for your career's success. Similarly, a red sofa set creates barriers at your workplace. Replacing the marble table for a wooden table and changing the color of your sofa set would help you overcome these problems.

- Light is a source of positive energy. Having enough lighting in the rooms is an important source of positivity. It is especially required for dull spaces where there are very windows receiving low amounts of sunlight. It is recommended you paint the walls with bright yellow, representing sunlight. If you are up for it, then painting the ceiling in a light yellow is also a great choice. You will have a very bright room, which is a great sign for feng shui.

- The bed should against a wall. Sleeping with your feet pointing towards the door is believed to be a well of negativity. This door can be the room door or also the direction of the main door. If you have a balcony then your feet should not point to that door either. So it is best that you find a place where your feet point to a wall. It is also recommended to remove any mirrors where you can see yourself lying in bed.

- The path from the door to the center of the room should be clear and not have any obstructions, like shoes or a bag. A clear doorway offers a clear flow of positive energy freely across the room. It is recommended you rearrange the seating arrangement in a way everyone in the room will be able to get a flux of positive energy.

- Place small mirrors in the room to help the amplification of positive energy throughout the area.

They improve the lighting of the room and also contribute to making the room look much larger than it actually is which makes it look comfortable. You can choose the wall that is directly opposite to a large window or a light source and place the mirror right in front of it. However, don't allow the mirror to face the door of the room. This can attract negative energy. Having a mirror on the wall in your bedroom should only be used if you are married and it is in the center of the ceiling where you can see yourself in bed.

- Plants and other flora are the living embodiments of nature. Surrounding your apartment with plenty of plants allows the healing energy vibrations of nature into your apartment. You need to take care of these plants to utilize the energies. Poor maintenance of these plants will bring out the negative energy held with dead and decaying plants.

- Water and fire elements do not integrate well. Their clash can be seen in daily life when a water element like a dishwasher, washing machine, refrigerator, or fish tank is placed opposite the stove or other heat source. You must avoid this clash as this could lead to family disagreements and competing interests attracting negative energies.

- Sleeping on the floor is never recommended as you're bound to be sick often. This is because of the poor flow of positive energy from the bottom. Hence, beds are beneficial for sleeping as the energy flows up. However, double bunk beds can cause more harm than good for the one who sleeps at the bottom. This is even more true if you have two children or more.

- Cluttering the house is the foundation for negative energy buildup. As the flow of positive energy is obstructed by disorder, there is loud negativity in the house/room. For the maintenance of an optimistic personality, the positive energy flow shouldn't be interfered with. Clutter has the worst effect when it is localized to the center of the room/house, which is regarded as the heart.

- Do not have an attic that is above your house. You will end up cluttering it and adding in a lot of elements.

This is a very negative energy, as you will feel burdened by all the clutter. Try not to have any form of attics including open shelves that are placed above head level.

- As it is a place where you lose the toxins from your body, keeping your bathroom clean is necessary. To be more careful, keeping the bathroom door closed at all times is the best way to contain and eliminate the negative energy. On a similar note, closing all doors of your apartment offers better health and improved sleep patterns.

Veronica Fujii

Chapter 6
Feng Shui Tips for Children's Rooms

When it comes to the children's room, it is important to keep in mind several factors, as you want to give your child the best that he or she can have in life. This includes giving them a nice place to crash at after a hard day's work and play.

Most people ignore children's rooms as they feel they will outgrow it in no time and that they will have to redo it again for them. However, they will not grow out of a room within a few months, and their rooms will have to remain the same for at least a few years. So simply giving them any room of your choice and expecting them to be happy with it is a bad decision. In fact, just by changing up the feng shui of the room, you can easily give your child the chance to do better not only in their schoolwork but also help increase their energy and productivity.

Here are some things you can bear in mind while designing your children's bedroom.

- Don't invest in bunk beds for your children. It is not good for the upper bed or the lower one, as they will have to bear a pressure. The person on top will have to bear the pressure of the ceiling and the child at the bottom has to feel the pressure of the bed on top. This can lead to a lot of discomfort between the two. Instead of this, you can choose to build a bed that turns into a study table, which will transform itself. This will not only save you space but having a ready structure installed will save you money and effort as well.

- Don't put the bed directly under a window, as that can be a bad thing. Have at least a two foot distance from the window and make sure the drapes are closed when the child is asleep. Do not place the bed in the opposite direction of the door, which means that they cannot see who is entering the room. The anticipation of knowing who might come in will make them uncomfortable.

- If you wish to install a carpet in the room, make sure that it goes under the bed or furniture and does not move. Pick geometric shapes and mild colors and try having a square or rectangle carpet as opposed to a round one.

- For a girl's room, try not having too many mirrors. It is understandable that girls love mirrors but don't have too many of them and try investing in just one large and fancy one. If she ends up breaking any one of the many mirrors then she might end up inviting bad luck. So make sure the mirror is small and hung on a wall that is not too close to other furniture. Avoid not having any mirror, however, as a full-length mirror that is placed in front of a window will help in increasing your child's self-confidence, and they will love to see themselves.

- You can buy a cute poster bed for your girl, as it is good feng shui. She will feel like a princess, and the posters will help trap in positive energy inside the structure of the bed. Light pink is the best color for your girl's bedroom regardless of how old she is. Baby pink will not just make her feel happy but is also a great feng shui color for a growing girl to be exposed to. Find light pink drapes and a light pink bed sheet that is either plain or has pink motifs on it.

- Mood lighting is a great choice as it can help your child relax. Have a few bright bulbs that can be switched on when the child is studying and some dim ones that will help them fall asleep. But there should be only about 5% light inside the room when they are asleep as any more can disturb them.

- The color blue is great for children's bedrooms, especially boys, and you can incorporate it in their room in any way that you like. This can include painting the walls blue or having key pieces of furniture such as the bed and the dressing table colored blue. Even drapes and bedspreads can be colored blue. But make sure it is light blue or even cyan and avoid any neon and bright colors as that can impact their psyche.

- Make sure there is a set place for all their toys as cluttered toys in the room is always bad feng shui. Teach them to add all their toys to the same box or closet on a daily basis and it will be a habit that will stick with them for life.

- Avoid having too many pictures and photographs hung inside the child's room. Have just a few small ones and neutral ones like you having a family time. If you hang up pictures of their achievements, then they will feel the pressure to deliver, and if they are not able to, then they will feel bad by looking at the picture.

- If your child is young then don't go ballistic if they end up drawing on the wall. You can always have it repainted. It is always great to give them a chalkboard to write on, and it is a good feng shui element to add to the room. It will promote education and keep your child interested in writing. You can also hang their drawings and other artwork, as it will up their productivity and inspiration.

- Make sure there is a big, bright window in the room as it helps to clean while fresh air moves in and out of the room. If you are moving into a new house, then take your child along and let them pick the room they want for themselves. You can then decorate it with them. Getting them to have a say is very important, and they will love making choices for themselves. Explain to them that you will supervise it as you are trying to increase their potential and then start installing elements of feng shui into their room.

- There should not be any beams on top in the children's room. If there is one, then change their room. Even masking the beam can allow negative energy to filter through.

- Having toys that keep moving or rock can invite negative energy. It can also scare the child. Make sure they are stowed away into the cabinet or cover them with a cloth so that they don't rock and scare the child when he or she is asleep.

- If there is a bathroom inside the children's bathroom then make sure the door automatically closes without having to close it manually. Leaving the door open when the child is sleeping is neither hygienic nor feng shui friendly.

Veronica Fujii

Chapter 7
Feng Shui Tips for the Garden

The garden is an area that is full of positivity, but you must make sure that the feng shui elements are in balance. There are many things to consider when decorating your garden and incorporating the various elements. It is not about buying pots and placing them in the sun; your garden needs a structure, and you have to consider several elements before deciding on a design. Let us look at the garden essentials you need to bear in mind for proper feng shui establishment.

- Always remember that there need to be structures and voids in your garden. This means that you have to have pots and plants, rocks, fountains, etc. and some voids such as empty spaces and pebbled walkways. You cannot have too many of one, and there needs to be a balance between the two elements. Plan it out in such a way that the plants surround the voids or the voids surround the plants.

- If you want your garden to last and the plants to remain healthy then you have to have fencing or a rock wall that runs around the garden. This rock wall does not have to be too fancy and can have a few rough edges. This will not just help your plants feel secure but you as well.

- Plan out the placement of your plants in such a way that they satisfy the feng shui colors in the direction that they are placed in. For example, the North loves the color blue, and so you can grow blue colored flowers in this direction. Similarly, grow red roses in the South direction to help increase the feng shui in this area of the garden. You can consult the Bagua map for further guidance. If you are not able to incorporate the color in the direction via the plants, then you can choose an element such as a chair that is colored and place it in the direction.

- Please make sure your plants and trees are exposed to only positive energy and nothing else. If they are exposed to negativity such as negative thoughts and people or even negative structures such as the gutter, then your plants are sure to be affected and may start dying. If you sing to your plants daily, then they will bloom and produce amazing flowers and fruits for you. You can also place a wind chime, which will chime sweetly and help your plants grow in a nice and serene environment.Always have a white flowering plant placed next to a colored plant. This will ensure that everything in your garden is well balanced. Some of the best white colored plants include water lilies, white roses, and plumeria. These plants are all perennials, and you won't have to worry about not having enough white color represented in your garden during certain months.

- Don't allow dead and decaying flowers and plants to remain in your garden, and get rid of them at the earliest. You must prune your plants from time to time and ensure that all the dead and dried leaves and flowers have been cleared away at the earliest moment possible.

- Don't clutter your gardening tools and make sure there is a set place for it. Have all of them neatly stacked in a box or hung on the wall. Make sure you clean them and don't allow any sand or mud to remain on them.

- It is not a good sign to have empty spaces or empty pots. Fill them up and make sure everything is full of plants at any given point in time. If you want a quick plant to grow then try a herb like mint as it will start to grow in bunches in no time at all.

- Remove all weeds from your garden from time to time. If you allow them to grow, then they will conflict with your plants and that can create some negative energy. Weed your garden every week and throw the plants as far as possible so that they don't get blown back into your garden due to the wind.

- Use a natural pesticide such as neem oil as chemical ones can create a lot of negative energy. Try using water sprays to get rid of pests such as aphids and mealy bugs and remove the affected leaves and stems as early as possible.

- If you have an indoor garden with indoor plants, then make sure they are all as far away from direct sunlight as possible. If they get any direct sun, then they will start to die, and that is not a good sign.

- If you want to add in a little color to your indoor garden then invest in orchids as they will not just add in an element of color but also aid in purifying the air inside your house.

- Incorporating a water feature in your garden is essential. It is also important that you place it in the right direction and that the water is in constant motion and not stagnating. The sound of the water will help your garden flourish.

Veronica Fujii

Chapter 8
Feng Shui Tips for the Bathroom

The bathroom is one place that is always ignored when it comes to feng shui. This is mainly because people associate negative energy with it, which means that they think it is a very bad place in the house and can cause a lot of negativity to flow out. This is not true. The bathroom has negativity no doubt but is not an evil place where monsters reside. You have to take care of the feng shui inside the bathroom as well and make sure that everything is in its rightful place. Here are bathroom feng shui tips that you can try out to better your bathroom and toilet space.

- Make your bathroom an experience. This will cut down on a lot of negativity. Invest your time and effort in creating an interesting ambiance in your bathroom. It is not important to make it extravagant, and all you need to do is increase the comfort and also help create a place that will instantly help your mind relax. For this, choose pastel colors such as light lavender, which will remind you of lavender flowers. Placing a few lavender flowers in a crystal vase next to the bathtub will also help you increase the serenity of the room.

- It is very important to introduce the element of wood inside the bathroom. The bathroom is a place where there is a lot of water flowing, which means there is an overload of the water element. Wood and other earth elements will balance it out, and you will have the chance to increase the décor inside the room. Invest in a wood cabinet, which can hold all your cosmetics and toiletries. You can also place a ladder made of wood next to the bathtub or the basin and hang all your hand towels and bath towels on it.

- If you are keen on balancing out all the elements in your bathroom, then you can have a fireplace installed as well. But this is only practical if you have enough space for it. If not, try placing a few candles and burn them when you are bathing.

- Make sure there is no clutter in the bathroom. Invest in some wicker baskets and make sure there is a place for everything. Having a lot of clutter is bad for your bathroom, and it will only increase the negative energy in the room.

- It is not possible to remove the negative energy from your toilet completely but is possible to decrease it a bit. To start off, place a small plant like a cactus on top of your water tank, as it will absorb some of the negative energy in the toilet.

- Placing something that smells good like potpourri or an aromatic candle in the bathroom can cut down the negative energy significantly.

- If you happen to have a bathroom in the money area of the house then invest in the color green as it is possible for you to increase the flow of money. So have green tiles and green paint and if possible, a green bathtub as well.

- It is not advisable to have a bathroom above the bedroom. You can try exchanging the bedroom with the living room if possible or else incorporate the element of wood and metal in your bedroom.

- It is possibly the worst set up ever to have a bathroom face your kitchen. Your negativity will be in such a flow that there will be just no end to it. However, to reduce its effects, you can always keep the door closed or if it is possible then create a door for it in an opposite room. Don't color both your kitchen and the bathroom in the same color; make sure to use two completely different palates..

Chapter 9

Feng Shui for a Senior Citizen's Room

While designing a room for a senior citizen, it is important to bear a few feng shui tips in mind. They are as follows.

- Minimalism is key. Get rid of all unwanted clutter and maintain a simple room. There should be nothing more than a simple bed, bedside tables, and a chair facing a window.

- There should be no television in the room, however, a transistor or a radio is fine.

- Use a pastel color for the walls like light green or light blue. Avoid using bright colors and also textures.

- It is important to dust every day and check for any mold and other such growth. It is essential that the senior citizen breathes in fresh air.

- You can incorporate a plant in the room but make sure it is low maintenance. You must not allow the water to stagnate in the plant and use a plate below the pot to catch the excess water.

- Making use of mood lighting is always great for senior citizens. Make use of pale yellow as it can help them relax better.

- The picture or idol of Buddha can be incorporated into the room to help them meditate. Have it hung on a wall that is on the side of their bed and make sure they do not point to the Buddha when they sleep.

- Placing a musical instrument in the room can increase the positivity in the room and also add in an element of metal. Choose something small like a ukulele for a small room or something even smaller like a flute, which can be hung on the wall.

- Make sure there is just one mirror that gets enough light coming in through the window.

Veronica Fujii

Chapter 10
Feng Shui Tips for the Garage

When it comes to feng shui, most people think it is for their bedroom or their living room. What they do not realize is how every room that is part of the house needs to be feng shui friendly. Most people only wish to use feng shui in their living spaces, but to be very honest the cupboard or the bathroom are not living spaces and yet they end up fixing the feng shui in these places. All the rooms will cumulatively contribute towards making the house fully feng shui friendly. In this chapter, we will look at the feng shui tips that you can adopt for your garage.

- At least 60% of people will use the garage as a place to store their clutter and junk. This is the worst thing to do, as it will invite a lot of negativity into your house. You must use the garage as nothing but a room to place your car and get rid of everything that is not needed.

- If you must store your things in the garage then invest in a few containers that can hold everything and make sure all of them are placed in a corner of the room.

- Paint your garage in a shade or green and don't neglect the walls. Dirty walls can invite bad energy, and you need to clean them from time to time. Similarly, you must clean the floors of the garage by making use of hot water and shampoo. Don't allow grease stains to remain and you can use sandpaper to sand it and remove the stains.

- Use the Bagua map and make sure everything in the garage is based according to it. Don't buy anything or remove anything until you have checked it out properly.

- It is a good idea to hang a painting or picture of a car that that is a bigger and better car than yours. It will invite good energy and chances are you will be able to afford that car some day.

- Make sure there is enough space for all the exhaust fumes to escape and allow fresh air to enter the garage.

- You have to try your best to prevent the garage door from making a sound, as it will invite a lot of negative energy. Oil it up from time to time to prevent the sound.

Veronica Fujii

Chapter 11
Feng Shui Tips for the Office

Your desk and office need just as much feng shui attention as your house. It is important that you grow career wise and improve your moneymaking capacity. If you have a cluttered office, then it will not be possible for you to make any progress. Here are some tips you need to bear in mind while designing your office to satisfy feng shui requirements.

- The first rule is to place the front desk right in front of the door. This door should be the door to your cabin. If this is not possible, then you can also place it facing the main door of the office. This will ensure that a lot of work comes your way, and you are always open to new clients. Choose a desk that is light and not too heavy. An all-wood desk is always a great choice for your office.

- Remember not to place your desk in front of another person's desk. This is bad energy, and your positivity will start to deplete.

- Get rid of all clutter in your office at the earliest possible time. Having organizational baskets that can hold all your things including documents and other knick-knacks are good. Don't rely on just your drawers to hold these, as your drawers will start to overflow in no time. Place the baskets under your desk.

- Having a small, fresh plant on your desk is always a good idea. It will help cleanse the air and also remove any negativity. You can choose a small indoor shrub such as vinca and water it regularly. Don't place cactus as that might invite negative energy. You can place some palms in the area behind your chair that is close to a window. Plants instantly increase the energy in a room and help increase the air of positivity. The plant should always be placed on the right-hand corner of the desk and nowhere else.

- Your desk, place your computer on the top left corner. The computer cannot be in the center, as it will block the positive energy. Don't pull it or push often and make sure that it stays there and is steadily installed.

- The center of the desk should be completely empty. There should be nothing including papers. Keep it as empty and free as possible. The top of the table next to the computer can have a set of visiting cards as that is a good place of communication, and you can have many contacts approach you.

- You can incorporate a small fountain on the desk or in your office but make sure it is in the southeast corner of the office. The flow of the water signifies the flow of wealth, and it will indicate that money is constantly flowing into your life. Clean the fountain once in a while and make sure the water is not moldy as that can be a bad sign.

- Light from the ceiling should always be flat. It should not be placed at an angle or have any dim color effect. It should not be placed directly above your head and can be a little this way or that.

- If there is more than one entrance to your office then close one permanently and place a potted plant in front of it. You can also place a couch in front of it to make sure nobody enters or exits from it.

- Having a wall behind you is always good. Don't sit in front of a window or a balcony door. Blue is a good wall color to have, and you can paint all the walls or you can paint three walls blue and allow one wall to remain white.

- Many people think that having a mirror on the wall in your office is a great way to make the office look spacious. However, it is important that you not have any mirrors inside your office as they can increase the negative energy in your office. Your clients can bring about this negative energy.

- Remember not to have any of the wires and cords in your office exposed or all jumbled up. You have to bunch them up and tie them using a cord or a rubber band.

- If you have a fish tank in the office make sure it is in the southeast corner. Feed them regularly and follow the rule of eight goldfish and one black fish to invite positive energy into your office.

- If the shape of your room is irregular, then that can mean bad feng shui. To fix it, you can make use of clear quartz. You can place a clear quartz pyramid in the office or suspend it from a string and hang it.

- The number 33 is considered to be very lucky in feng shui. You can write that down on a piece of paper and place it in your desk drawer.

- If there is a pole or a beam in the room then you must place a plant under or below it to cut out the negativity in the room. Don't place your desk or your chair under it, as it will increase the pressure on you.

- If you are in a cubicle or have to share office desk and space with someone else then you can place the picture of a water fountain if you cannot place a real one. Place a smaller plant like a lucky bamboo and reduce the amount of clutter present on your cubicles desk.

- Many people prefer to place their family pictures on the desk, but this is not a good thing. It can cause you to get distracted. Even if you want to have a picture then make sure it is small and not too big. Don't have too many knick-knacks and try and keep it minimalist.

- You can join three metal coins, with a hole in the center, using a red ribbon and place it in your desk drawer. This will ensure that positive energy flows in and a steady cash flow is maintained.

Chapter 12
Feng Shui Tips for the Bedroom

The bedroom is one place where you would want to have good feng shui. It is necessary that there is a balanced flow of energy. This energy rejuvenates you and nourishes your aura.

Your bedroom is the one place you would want to go to after you have had a terrible day at work or school. You find your bedroom inviting and feel a calm spreading through your body at the same time. If you have a room with good feng shui, you will find that it is pleasant to stay in the room. This chapter deals with the tips that you can use to ensure that you have a balanced bedroom.

Remove Every Electronic Gadget

You have to ensure that your bedroom does not have any electronic gadgets. The vibrations from these gadgets create an imbalance to the chi in your room. Make sure that your laptop and your cell phone are anywhere but near the vicinity of your bedroom. Have a set place for your cell phones like the living room and place them in a basket so that the negative energy is all trapped inside the basket and does not leave it.

Remove all the Exercising Equipment

The exercise equipment is a constant reminder of the fact that you are not fit and are trying to reach your goal. You do not want to be haunted by that fact when you are in your bedroom. This equipment tends to drain all the good energy away. Try to have a separate room for all this equipment. Let it not be anywhere close to your bedroom! It is best not to have a home gym in your living room but inside your basement.

Open Windows

It is always good to have the windows open. Leave them open throughout the day. Shut them before the mosquitoes enter the room, though. The windows act as your very own energy attractor. They help in letting in all the good energy. They also help in removing any bad energy that is found in your room. You can have an air freshener or an air purifier in your room. This will help you cleanse the air. Make sure that the freshener is scented with your favorite smell. This helps in spreading a calm energy through your body.

Great Lighting

The lighting in your room plays a very important role in feng shui. You need Vitamin D, which is obtained only from the sunlight. Light is also an element that is closely related to the fire element. This element ensures that there is a good amount of happy energy in your life. When you have minimal light flowing into your room, you will tend to become gloomy. You may wake up with dread or fear every morning. But if your room is full of light, you will be able to wake up with a bright smile on your face.

Basic Tips

The basic tips that you will need to follow are:

- Make sure that your bed is approachable to you from both sides and that you can enter and exit it from both sides
- Ensure that there is a table on each side of the bed as it helps balance out the room. It can be a small table, but there should be two and not just one
- Make sure that there are night lamps on the tables and not too many things that you get lost looking for something that you need
- Ensure that the sheets that you use on your bed are colorful and vibrant and break the habit of having just white sheets
- Make sure that you have a good number of windows in your room that point to each other as this will ensure there is a lot of cross ventilation inside the room

Chapter 13
Feng Shui Tips for the Kitchen

The kitchen is where you work on nourishing your family. You cook different foods that provides nourishment to your family. This food is what helps you sustain the life of your family.

When you look at your kitchen from the perspective of feng shui, you will find that the kitchen is the essence of your house. In the feng shui theory, the kitchen is where you generate great wealth and prosperity. It is best to have the kitchen indoors and not on the outside of your house. If it is on the outside of your house, you are letting your wealth and prosperity flow right out the window.

The kitchen is where you prepare food that helps you fill yourself with a good amount of energy. You have to ensure that your kitchen is filled with good energy and a brilliant flow of that energy. You will need to ensure that the kitchen is organized in such a way that there are no blockages of any kind.

This chapter covers a few tips that you could use to feng shui your kitchen.

Proper Lighting

The lighting in your room plays a very important role in feng shui. You need Vitamin D, which is obtained only from sunlight. Light is also an element that is closely related to the fire element. This element ensures that there is a good amount of happy energy in your life. When there is no sunlight, you will find that the fruits and the vegetables that you use for cooking have lost their sheen and color. You have to ensure that there is a good amount of light energy in the kitchen at all times.

Spacious Kitchen

There has to be a good amount of space in the kitchen. There have to be a lot of drawers at home and also a good number of hooks in the kitchen. This will ensure that you have enough space to move around. You could have the gas stove in the middle of the kitchen and have all the drawers and windows around it. Ensure that there is a good amount of space between the stove and the utensils. If you have an island, then see if removing the island can help you create more space in your kitchen. If it is possible to take down a wall like a balcony wall and increase space of the kitchen, then you can do that.

Airy

There has to be a good amount of air in the kitchen. Ensure that there are a lot of windows in the kitchen. This will ensure that there is a good flow of energy in the kitchen. If you don't have enough windows, then you can invest in a good ventilation system and make sure all the bad air exits the room.

Clean

Make sure that the countertops and the kitchen floor are always clean. When you have a dirty environment, you tend to have a life that is not as clean as you would want it to be. Make sure that there is a lot of brightness in your kitchen! Paint the walls a bright color. The best colors for the kitchen include orange and yellow. You can also try the color blocking technique where the wall that lies directly in front of the window is painted a light color so that it reflects the light and the rest of the walls are slightly darker. Do not color the insides of cabinets in colors that are dark. It should be light and preferably white.

Chapter 14
Decluttering

One of the ways to absorb the good feng shui energy is through proper clutter management. Clutter and waste accumulation serves as a barrier between you and your prosperity in life. A consistent flow of chi assists in the development of good fortune in life. Your good fortune could easily turn into bad luck if you do not manage your clutter wisely. There are certain items in your house that you no longer have any use for, such items could take up the larger amount of space and cause an obstruction in the accommodation of your useful items. Reducing clutter can help you invite good feng shui into your home or workplace.

Sort Your Mail Instantly

Daily mail could clutter when left unchecked. Unpaid bills of all kind don't just accumulate and cause stress, but they also clutter and harm the flow of chi. To get the most of feng shui's energies, screen and sort your mail as soon as it arrives in a regulated manner. Apart from bills and mail, ensure there are no cluttering sheets or documents at home. Categorizing and neat arranging of the useful documents and throwing away of the ones that are no longer of use should benefit you.

Clean Daily

If your cleaning schedule involves cleaning only on weekends, then your home/workplace will not have any positive energy flow. Instill the habit of cleaning on a regular basis and you will soon find yourself free of clutter. It will be most useful when you clean your home regularly. Your daily cleaning doesn't have to be vigorous, light efficient cleaning will serve you better. But you also have to declutter the house on a monthly basis and get rid of all the things that you do not need at all. You can start by having three boxes named "keep" "donate" and "throw". Add all the keep items to the keep box, the donating items to the donate box and the throw items to the throw box. Empty the boxes accordingly.

Clean As You Work

While working on a project, clean as you go. This means that you will not just leave stuff lying around on the table as you do your work. This ensures that the workspace remains clean, and this also implies that you are open for more productive work in the future since the space is wiped free of any traces from previously done work.

Generosity

Charity begins at home. This applies for your clutter too. Give away stuff that is no longer of use for you with a generous attitude. It is always possible that the items you consider as waste are important for others. Although items like old papers and bills aren't useful for others, and you may end up transferring clutter. Always check for the condition and purpose of what you are donating. You can ask a family member if they want something from you. Don't simply hold on to it just because someone else wants it; part with it and forget about it. You will feel happy for having helped someone and they will be grateful for having gotten it from you.

Dust Frequently

Remove the dust that accumulates on windows, tables, and other places through frequent dusting. This will help you keep the place neat and tidy. A large amount of dust build-up contributes to clutter. Have a set time in mind when you wish to dust a room. Don't think you will do it today or do it tomorrow, etc. If you have set the time as Saturday morning, then make sure you do it at that exact time. Some people prefer to dust every day, this is important if you live in a dusty space. Set a time such as 8 pm and make sure you start dusting at 8 pm sharp.

Be Brutal

When it comes to evaluation of an item, either take the advice of a peer or be strict when it comes to the clearance. When you refuse to part with an item that you've had for many years and have developed a sense of affection to it, it is a sign of bad feng shui. Such items can clutter and cause problems. Therefore, it is important for you to be brutal when it comes to decluttering.

Veronica Fujii

Chapter 15
Feng Shui Tips for the Living Room

It is essential that you have good feng shui in your living room. The feng shui in the living room is based on the same energy principles as the feng shui for the entire house. You have to ensure that the living room is clean and has absolutely no clutter in it. Before you begin the feng shui transformation in your living room, it is best for you to declutter. Follow the principles and tips that have been provided above to help you remove any clutter in the living room. A clutter creates a blockage in the flow of the energy. This is the minimum that is required to ensure that you have a good flow of energy in your living room. This chapter covers the simplest tips to incorporating feng shui in your living room.

Clear Organization

You have to ensure that you follow a system of organization in your living room. You will need to specify that certain areas in the living room are only for certain objects. If you fail to do this, you will have a tough time trying to ensure that your living room is arranged based on the theories of the feng shui. You may find it exceedingly difficult when you have children at home. But the truth is that these children can help you keep your living room organized. All you have to do is tell them what the rules are and communicate effectively.

Choose a Good Décor

This requires a lot of planning and a lot of work! First, you will have to try to understand what the feng shui theories are and also what you will need to do in the different areas in your house. There is a theory called the Bagua, which helps you create a map for your entire house. This map determines the flow of energy, which will help you identify the areas where you have to avoid adding any décor for fear of blocking the energy. When you learn the different feng shui areas in your living room, you can begin by choosing the colors that will enhance the feng shui. You have to pick materials in the same way too! If you already have a heavily decorated room then plan out how you can reduce it and have only a few key pieces present in the room. You can take a picture of your room and use an app that will help you get rid of some pieces virtually so that you will know exactly what to keep and what to get rid of. Don't end up doing away with good pieces and plan out everything before taking action. When you wish to choose a place for the television and the entertainment center, you have to make sure that all your sofas and couches point to it. You will also want to make sure that it is possible to view television from every area of the room. This is important as otherwise there will be fights for the best seat in the house.

Incorporate All Five Feng Shui Elements

You will have to ensure that the five elements theory is followed strictly. You will need to arrange the furniture in such a way that there is an uninhibited flow of energy through the entire living room. You must never block a window using a cupboard. Try to ensure that there is enough light that is entering the room. Leave the windows open to ensure that there is a good amount of air circulation. It is only through this air that you can ensure that there is a good flow of energy. This will help you create a warm, social, and comfortable living room using the feng shui theories.

It is important that you follow the guidelines that have been mentioned above. You may follow them word for word but you have to remember that this is your house that you are decorating! You will need to choose décor and paint that you have a feeling will suit your house. Do not go only by what is said here! When you use feng shui, you are creating a home that has a good amount of energy, which nourishes you, thereby making you happy and content. You may have read through different tips and tricks that you could use. But you have to remember to do what you love! Only you know what makes you most happy. Allow yourself to provide a happy, warm and a welcoming home for yourself and for your family.

Chapter 16
The Benefits of Feng Shui

Feng shui advantages fascinate most people, and there are several reasons for it. To beginners, feng shui might seem like a superstitious interior design practice but as you understand the significance of positive energy and homogeneity between you and your surroundings, the definition of feng shui gets more complicated. Feng shui is an integration of studies from various schools of learning and stays true to the different cultures under which it is housed.

The best part of feng shui is that it can be understood easily and implicated by a layman into a home without having to spend too much. Apart from that, there are other advantages that can only be felt once you embrace feng shui into your life.

Psychological Benefits

The feeling of coming home to your own apartment should drive away all the stress that accumulates in the day. Your mind and body should feel lighter, energetic, self-satisfied, and content. If this is not the case, and you come home restless, tired, sloppy, overwhelmed, and irritated rather than the optimistic feeling you had in the morning, then you and your family could benefit from embracing feng shui. Your body and mind will experience a sense of stability within which will have a positive effect on your family all through feng shui.

The human mind is extremely complex and works in ways that is beyond understanding. However, it is easy to know that a clutter free environment that allows fresh air to flow freely is a great mental relaxant. With the amount of stress that people take up these days, it is next to impossible not to feel stressed. But the easiest way to beat this stress is by having the most relaxing bedroom environment that will not just eliminate your stress but also keep those midnight blues at bay.

To balance your mind, you must remove the clutter in your home as well as reduce the clutter in your mind, which will allow you to calm down and make chi flow freely and smoothly. This improves your decision-making skills making it easier for your take decisions. Make sure you are not simply moving the clutter from one place to another. You will end up wasting your effort and return to zero again. You should also consider the concept of colors, which affect your mood and are specific to the personalities of your family members. When positive energy flows through all the members of a family, it improves the mental feng shui presiding over your home. The vibrations from the proper flow of chi in your apartment can even heal psychological ailments within your mind.

Environmental Benefits

Adding plants and flora to a room isn't exactly a feng shui concept but when you add an earth element like plants they offer stability to your home. This establishment of balance promotes the growth of your home and family both physically and mentally. There are also air-purifying plant species, which are a part of the earth element that can purify the air you breathe. According to research conducted by NASA, indoor pollutants contain more impurities than outdoor pollutants, and the only way to eliminate these impurities is through plants. These air-purifying plant species are the Pygmy Date Palm (*Phoenix roebelenii*), Areca Palm (*Dypsis lutescens*), Kimberly Queen Fern (*Nephrolepis obliterata*), Variegated Snake Plant/Mother-In-Law's Tongue (*Sansevieria trifasciata 'Laurentii'*), Red-Edged Dracaena (*Dracaena reflexa var. angustifolia*), etc. Just by placing these plants in your house you can easily get rid of toxins and carbon monoxide. These can come into the house through many sources including vehicle fumes and the various chemicals that your house cleaners emit. Placing them near the bathrooms will also help you get rid of these chemical fumes. If you have a burnt smell coming from the oven from leftover food drying up on the gas grates, you can place a few plants in the kitchen and get rid of the smell as well as the burnt fumes. Plants like Dumb Cane (*Dieffenbachia)* will do the trick.

Stability in Life

If you find yourself stressed and burdened with clutter accumulating all over your home and workplace, you will find the practice of feng shui most beneficial. If you suffer from cases of visual imbalance in your life with respect to your surroundings, feng shui will be the ideal way to introduce balance into your life by incorporating certain components that allow you to control the environment around you. If you achieve stability in life through minor things like furniture arrangement, you are bound to attain a greater sense of stability in other aspects of life. You will not believe it, but these things really do help people. They allow you to lead a better life and increase your productivity potential. They will not only cause you to improve your physical stability but your mental stability as well. So don't think picking cane furniture will not help your mental state as anything that is natural will definitely up your spirit and just by sitting on it, you will have the chance to connect with nature. This stability of both mind and body is crucial for all human beings.

Mindfulness

Being aware of minor things in life is always a good thing. When you're heavily focused on the larger concept of stability in life, you miss out on the minute details, which signify the importance of the art of living. Minute details like the home arrangement and maintenance of the environment. If they are ignored in the background, they tend to decay in the background building up to a high-stress environment which can lead to several other problems and worries in life. Mindfulness is a great tool to use to beat stress in your life. You will be aware of the various small things around you that help in maintaining a focus. If you are tensed or worried about something then focusing on something as simple as the color of the wall will help you relax and get over something. Don't worry if you get lost in the elements of feng shui. You will only come out feeling fully rejuvenated and feeling fully at peace with your life and your situation. You will have a better capacity for dealing with life's issues and stresses.

The Feng Shui Community

As you embrace feng shui into your life, you get to meet several feng shui experts and enthusiasts. By meeting new people, communicating with others, and sharing your experiences you will think of feng shui as more than a superstition. There are also chances in the feng shui community that you will end up finding another member within your network who has a similar taste as you and help you with any feng shui developments, no matter how insignificant. It is always fulfilling to be a part of something big and great. It is possible for you to explore the depths of the craft. You will also have the chance to contribute towards it in a big way. And by embracing something that is good for all you will help in spreading the message. Remember that someone else benefitting from feng shui practice after hearing from you or looking at your practices will not just help them but also help you, and you will partake in their benefits as well. So not only will you benefit from your investment in it but also from their investment in it.

A Fresh New Perspective

A new perspective on old things is always welcome as it makes you feel fresh and bright. The perspective, however, should be a positive one as that invites changes in your daily life schedule for the greater good. Feng shui serves as a fresh new perspective to interior design and home arrangement, ultimately benefitting you in the long run. The benefits of feng shui contribute to the enrichment of one's mind, body, and soul. You don't always need to stick with modern designs and can go with a more rustic theme from time to time. You will have the chance to explore the science, and it will make for a very interesting subject to teach your children. They will also be surprised with the number of alternate sciences that exist in the world and how it is possible for them to partake in it. You can also get your friends involved in it and teach them a thing or two about exploring the alternate world of science.

Prosperity and Success

The main objective of embracing feng shui is to attain stability and prosperity in life. When you are prosperous and balanced, success will be yours. We saw how it is not just easy for you to fulfill your needs and ambitions but also lead a smooth life. Just by making a few different arrangements in your office space you can modify how something works in your favor. You are not required to change up everything, and all you have to do is add a few elements. You cannot just grow career wise but also make a lot of money owing to changing up a few elements inside the room.

Aesthetic Appeal

A feng shui home is extremely beautiful as symmetry is involved in the positioning of all your objects. This gives an aesthetic appeal to your home and the surrounding environment. There is a physical appeal to a well-decorated home and with integrated feng shui techniques; your home could also have a mental appeal to it with a positive flow of energy all through. Feng shui promotes beauty in both physical and mental forms of life.

The Twenty Simplest Benefits of Feng Shui

You have read about the different ways in which feng shui benefits you. But this section deals with the benefits that will appeal to you in many ways.

- You will be able to get a job or a raise or a promotion with ease
- You will be able to improve your health
- You will find it easier to get a partner for yourself or get married
- Pregnancy becomes easier for you, you will also be able to avoid miscarriages
- You will be able to guard yourself against separating or divorcing your partner
- You will feel motivated at every step in your life
- There will be more harmony at your home and work
- If you are a student, you will find that you are able to study better
- You will have a great boost in your creativity
- You will find yourself feeling more in control
- You will find control in your office and your house as you will find that you are able to avoid any imbalances in the way you feel
- You will be able to eliminate depression
- Your social life will become vibrant

- If you own a business, you will find it flourishing in ways you had never imagined before
- You will be able to prevent anything happening to you on the legal front You will also find that you are able to avoid any malicious influences
- You will be able to prevent any accidents from occurring
- If you require new areas for shelter, you will be able to find them with ease
- You will be able to ward off any addictions
- You will find that you do not suffer from insomnia
- Respect and fame will find their way to you

You may have the feeling that your life is right on track, but there is no harm in practicing feng shui. You will be able to benefit from this in many other ways. You can have fun with feng shui! Get your friends and your family to try it!

Veronica Fujii

Chapter 17
Feng Shui for Stress Relief

Feng shui home décor is an art. Each of the individual components like the lighting, the furniture, the artwork, and the colors all need to be balanced to achieve perfect harmony between your home and the environment that surrounds you.

A harmonious place doesn't just involve matching the drapes with the carpet or applying the perfect linens all around the house. It involves designing a place that is calming not only to the eye but also to the soul. Your home's décor should be constructed in a manner, which allows the flow of positive energy into the house contributing to the reduction of anxiety levels and bring out the inner harmony of nature. All of this is possible through a conceptual design that complies with feng shui principles.

The main causes for excessive stress are major energetic unbalance that presides over your home and workplace. Your environment plays a larger part in your life than you think it does. Whenever you've felt down and out, stressed and unmotivated, poor sleep patterns, and then the reason or contributing factor for this scenario is your environment.

According to most feng shui enthusiasts, the only way to get relief from the stress buildup is to create a sense of balance. A balance needs to be found between the Five Elements of the earth, that are water, earth, metal, wood, and fire. For example, a home with too much of the fire element can lead to a stressful environment. Similarly, an improperly designed space can cause issues, which involve more anxiety and stress in your life. To curb stress levels, you will have to balance the elements, colors, correct your furniture positioning and orientation, and even clean out the clutter developing in each room of your house, giving your home a feng shui makeover.

The Entrance

The entrance is one of the most important areas of the house as it is where positive energy comes in and disperses throughout the house. To ensure that the energy emerging is good energy, it is crucial to eliminate all clutter accumulation, soften any sharp and crooked design items, or substitute it for curved shaped furniture encouraging the sideward flow of energy. If your entrance is a little compact, you can expand that little space by placing a portrait or artwork, which represents infinity like an ocean, a desert, a meadow and others. Alternatively, perpendicularly hung mirrors with respect to the door have a similar effect. For the main entrance of the house, it is best that you choose the north or northeast direction. This direction brings in both luck and prosperity. It is important that your main door does not open up to a road or a staircase, and it is slightly offset. But if it is then you can place a Buddha statue in front of the door. If there is a staircase that goes up and is placed right in front of your main door then you can place a mirror on top of the door. This will counteract the negative energy that comes from the staircase. You can also place a fish tank a short distance from the main door that will counteract the negative energy that flows in. Again, you have to have eight goldfish and a black one which is a great feng shui combination. Having one koi is also good but don't place it in a small tank as it should be big enough for the fish to move around freely.

The Bedroom

Designing the bedroom to deliver a stress-free environment is crucial as it is the room where you rest, where you sleep. It also has to be the most peaceful room in the house to ensure your sound sleep. Apart from that it also has to be motivating and full of positive energy as you start every morning in that room. For absorbing a maximum of positive energy and easing your stress in life, it is advised that you position the bed far from the door. Moreover, sleeping on the floor isn't recommended as it blocks the flow of energy beneath you when you sleep.

When you're in your bedroom, your energy is open and exposed to your surroundings making you very vulnerable in the bedroom. It is important you retain the energy in the room hence it is recommended you keep the furniture like bookshelves to a minimum. When you accumulate your bedroom with stuff like electronics, books, or important documents it leads to a lot of stress. In this information age, it is impossible to get entirely rid of the electronic devices. However, you could put them on silent mode so that your sleep is not disturbed ensuring maximum stress relief.

It is always advisable to get rid of all idols and pictures of gods from your bedroom. It is a place where you sleep and also have some bonding time with your partner. So it is not a good place for you to place a god's idol and expose it to all of these activities. Just make sure you remove them and place them in an appropriate corner. For all those who take it seriously, the west direction is a good place to place your god and so is the south. You can have a small bench or a wall stand where you can place the idol or the picture.

The Home Office

Your workplace is a major hotspot for clutter. Clutter is vicious; it comes in many forms and is a significant source of stress. Especially in your workplace, all the old documents, worksheets, and pending reports could lead to immense amounts of stress. For proper stress management, install a good filing system that arranges your clutter and organizes it correctly. If you experience problems with your organization skills, you might have too many earth elements like stones or earthy colors painted on the walls of the room. You will need to stabilize it and balance the earth elements with metal elements like sculptures or metallic colors painted on walls.

A crucial factor in your workplace's feng shui is the positioning of your desk. Your desk should be placed in a way that your back is against a solid wall without any windows. As per feng shui, you would be inviting stress at your workplace if you sit with your back facing a door. Hence, positioning of your desk properly is of extreme importance.

Apart from the clutter and furniture arrangement, the lighting also affects the mental peace of the individuals in the room. The fluorescent lighting with its unnatural light spectrum, mild humming noise, and consistent flickering all create an environment, which is uneasy and felt out of place.

The Living Room

The living room, just like any other room in the house, will benefit from a spectrum of bright colors. Avoid colors like orange, red, and black for the large area and opt for softer shades of yellow, pink, green, and white. However, you should avoid painting blue on any of the walls of the living room as in feng shui it is believed to be an unwelcoming color.

The right orientation and shape of the furniture in the space of the living room also contributes to stress relief and peace of mind. The furniture should be in proportion to the room size and not humongous which can take up more space and interrupt the circulation of chi. Similarly, round or curvy designs are recommended as they mimic nature to the best extent. These shapes are more natural when compared to sharp, straight lines.

Décor, to a certain extent, contributes to a healthy energy flow. However, over-decorating with several accessories, especially too many small items like photos don't just take up a lot of space but also create chaos. Bring down the decorations to items that have a calming background to them like photos of your vacation. Alternatively you can include a floral component to the living room to reduce the stress levels.

The Kitchen

An ideal feng shui design for a kitchen is the popular triangular layout where the stove, refrigerator, and sink are positioned at three ends to form a triangular shape. This arrangement does take huge capital and time to implement, but it is crucial as this room is where food, which is fed to the members of the family, is prepared.

If your kitchen isn't suitable for this arrangement, you can consider shifting your appliances such that the stove is adjacent to the sink, dishwasher, or refrigerator. If they are opposite to each other, this could lead to a clash of fire and water elements which isn't good. It is also recommended you keep your fridge and cabinets almost full at all times as it will represent wealth and abundance.

Every individual has a unique perspective and a personal taste and to find a feng shui layout, which suits you, may be hard. You will have to be prepared to compromise on a few aspects like embracing colors of a more relaxing palate or to rearrange few pieces of your furniture around, all this will benefit you a consistent positive energy flow.

Veronica Fujii

Chapter 18
Secret Ways to Improve Your Feng Shui

This chapter covers the secret tips that you will have to use to ensure that the feng shui that you have in your house benefits you in all ways! These are not tips but the Bible to feng shui. You will need to follow them word for word to ensure that you improve on your feng shui.

Find Ways to Add Beauty to Your Home or Workplace

This is one of the most important tips! It is essential that you beautify your house or your workplace to your liking. This will ensure that you enjoy doing what you do at home and at work.

You could use different books on home décor and on workplace décor. You can even use pictures that bring a smile to your face. Hang them on the walls at home. Take a few of them and place them on your desk at work. You can use bright colors at home and also beautify your home with different types of furniture. You can have different mementos that you may have collected on your travels garnishing the shelves in the living room in your house.

Remove the Negative Energy From Your Environment

You will have to remove any negative energy that you have around you. You will find that this negative energy is essentially bad for you since it always clouds any positive energy that may enter your environment.

If there are objects that remind you of any negative things, ensure that you remove them from your life this very instant. These objects could be pictures or gifts or even people. Sometimes there are people you are very close to who tend to hurt you or remind you of a certain negative memory. Try to stay away from them. This will help you ensure that you have a good amount of positive energy around you.

This is the same at work too. There are times when you find it difficult to work in a certain environment. Try to get rid of the place immediately. You will have to work to finding a new job but do it! Ensure that you are doing what you like and in a place where you like. You should try to be like Holly from *P.S I Love You*. She goes out of her way to find a job that she genuinely loves. Had she done that before, she would not have felt the need to complain to her husband every night about how terrible her day at work had been. Do you think that is true? Think about it. It may not seem the right thing to do, but try to take some time off and see what works best for you.

Declutter, and do it quick!

This is a mantra that you have to follow! In the series, '*The Shopaholic*', Rebecca Bloomwood shops her way into debt. She feels that she needs to buy a certain item if it is on sale. She does not stop to think about whether or not she needs it.

She jumps up at the opportunity to buy clothes or shoes or even a bag! This is not what you should do. You have to ensure that you only buy things that you need. When you are working on feng shui, you will have to ensure that you do not have any object that you do not need.

When you are going grocery shopping, make a list for yourself and stick to the list! It is essential that you stick to the list! It is only this way that you will be able to ensure that you have no clutter at home.

Balance the Environment Around You

You have to ensure that there is a good amount of balance in the energy around you. There will have to be equal amounts of positive and negative energy. If you find an imbalance, try to change the way you have arranged your furniture. You may also find an imbalance when there is a bad arrangement of the windows or the objects at home.

Good Alignment

It is essential that you align yourself to the good directions. It is said that you must never place your head towards the south when you are sleeping. You could try to ensure that your head is in the east or west since these are the best places to align your head when you sleep. The north is said to be the direction of the devil, and so, it is important that you not face this direction when you are sleeping lest you end up seeing the devil in your dreams! This alignment ensures that you do not have any issues with insomnia or any bad dreams.

You also have to ensure that when you arrange the furniture in the living room you have to move everything along the lines of good energy. You have to be like Sheldon Cooper from '*The Big Bang Theory*'. You have to find the best place for yourself at home. He ensures that he is able to watch the television and talk to his friends at the same time. He also mentions the draft of wind. This is what you have to make sure you have in your position. This can be done even at work.

Never Sit Under Beams

You should never sit under the beams. You must ensure that you never lie down under them either. There is a certain amount of pressure that the beams exert on the energy that is flowing into the room. There may have been times when you have sat under a beam and have found yourself complaining about how your head felt heavy. You may have never realized that there was a beam right above you. But this is the only reason for the heaviness. To avoid such a feeling, try to avoid sitting or sleeping under beams. If you don't have a choice in your house and have too many beams, then try to use space wisely. Move the furniture from underneath it and place it elsewhere. It is best to leave the space under it completely empty or place something that is not used much like a side table or just a table. Don't sit near the table and use it to place something on instead. If it is not the main beams and something that can be removed then speak with your architect or engineer and tell him you want the beam removed from there.

Never Leave Anything Broken

If you find that there are cracks in the driveway get them fixed immediately. You do not want the energy to seep through these cracks. If you have any broken objects, get rid of them immediately. You do not want your life to attract any negative energy. If you can fix them, do that immediately. If a crack still prominently shows on the object then don't keep it. If by any chance you have gifted someone something that is broken then don't accept it back, ask them to discard it and give them something else that is proper and free from cracks and damages. Although there is a lot of superstition against broken mirrors, don't panic if a mirror breaks or cracks simply discard it and don't fuss over it.

Involve Yourself With Feng Shui

This is the last tip of the book! You will need to join communities on the Internet or join support groups. You will find that you are able to obtain better ideas on how to arrange your house. You will also be able to ensure that you have a good amount of energy flowing through your entire home! You will be able to use feng shui to enhance your way of living!

Veronica Fujii

Chapter 19
Frequently Asked Questions on Feng Shui

This book is a comprehensive book that throws abundant light on the practical use of feng shui. Reading this book can also sometimes overwhelm you and this section gives you a brief idea on feng shui. The questions that are asked here are common questions and it is important to note that some questions may be repetitive, and you may have found the answers when reading this book. However, I hope it clarifies all your doubts and queries.

Is Feng Shui considered to be really effective?

Practicing the art of feng shui is known to be very effective.

Research and studies have been conducted, and they have all given positive results about practicing feng shui. Feng shui has a positive impact on the environment and on the people in living in that particular surrounding. If you do your own research, there are also several people who swear by this ancient art. It leads to a well-balanced life and helps to attract good energy and reduced bad energy. It is also an ancient art and has been practiced for centuries and that proves that it has been effective.

Can anybody practice Feng Shui?

Anyone can take up feng shui. Feng shui is a form of discipline and can have a positive impact on your life and it is not restricted by the various aspects and boundaries. You also don't need to be an expert to practice this. Start by reading a few books and browsing the Internet. There are also communities and groups both online and offline for feng shui enthusiasts that you can join to get more ideas on feng shui.

Is Feng Shui considered to be sustainable?

Feng shui is very effective, and the results do stay for a long period and hence they are long lasting. However, it is better to check and test the energy flow within the place to ensure positive energy flow at all times. Usually, you wouldn't have to make further changes when changes are once made. Thus it is highly sustainable.

Is Feng Shui expensive?

Feng Shui can be both expensive as well as cost effective depending on many factors. The expenses incurred often include the consultation fee and the various tools and equipment that you will need to secure your house with positive energy. To reduce the costs, you can browse the Internet for tips or get books that will help you give an idea on what you should be doing for good feng shui. Other expenses that you might incur include the course of action that you need to take, the paintings, the shifting of things, and so on.

Does every house have a wealth corner?

In every house there exists one particular place that, when decorated properly, enables prosperity and growth of wealth. This is found by a few measurements, for more details view the chapter on this.

Does there exist an easy and simple way to identify the wealth corner present in a house?

No, there isn't any easy or simple way to identify the wealth corner that is present in your house. It is best not to go about the easy ways that are present on the Internet. This is important because there are times when following a short cut might lead to adverse effects.

Is Lo Pan important for the application of Feng Shui?

The Chinese compass called the Lo Pan is very important for the applications of feng shui. It helps to make the correct estimations and helps to calculate the distances. Alternately any accurate compass can also be used in place of the Lo Pan.

How long do results take to appear?

Results can vary depending on many factors. For one, feng shui can start working in your life within a few days of implementation. Generally, feng shui shows improved results within a few weeks or a month. Again, this is not the case with everyone; there are times when it can take a longer time. It also depends on the amount of changes that you make. Making many changes immediately is always a good idea. It also depends on what kind of results you are looking for. If you are looking for personal gain and success it can take a little time based on the way the way you, your environment, and those around you interact. However, the key thing to remember here is that feng shui is effective and it will definitely show results when practiced properly.

Does Feng Shui require a master to learn it or can it be learnt without one?

You don't need a master or a professional to teach you how to practice feng shui. The point is it is easier to learn through as a master as opposed to reading a lot of feng shui books that may have contradictory statements. Traditionally, feng shui was learnt using and referring to several books so if you have the time and patience you should go ahead. There are also feng shui courses online to help you.

Is it true that all kinds of mirrors are powerful weapons to kill negative energy?

This is not true. Mirrors are reflective surfaces that reflect the light that falls onto it. Mirrors do not absorb nor do they disperse any bad energy.

Can Feng Shui help you gain prosperity and bring you wealth?

Feng shui certainly can help in that aspect. Practicing feng shui will not lead to an abundance of wealth but it will create a positive environment for you where you can harness the positive energy to your use. It helps in clarifying a person's mind, bringing peace and harmony. It also promotes health, good thinking, and wisdom. Thus, it can aid in a person using his or her talents, abilities, and capabilities in making money.

How can one read Feng Shui?

A person who practices feng shui or reads feng shui does it by using a particular Chinese compass called Lo Pan. This compass will help determine the type of energy of a place and how that energy affects the people in that place. Apart from just using the compass several calculations and analysis are based using the feng shui principles. The person then gives ideas on how things should be placed or what course of action can be taken to have a peaceful comforting aura around the place.

Do toilets hinder wealth, health, and marriage?

Toilets are generally considered to be dirty places. It contains so many microorganisms that can cause numerous ailments and diseases. Toilets should be located in a remote location and must be flushed after every use. They should also be clean and hygienic and be maintained properly. This is not just attributed to feng shui but general cleanliness as well. Like the old saying goes, cleanliness is godliness. Toilets do not have any impact on the wealth. This belief probably comes because when someone is sick, lot of money is spent on that person to help them recover.

The plants at my home all get dried or wither and die. Does this happen because of bad Feng Shui?

It is important to note that all life forms are connected and have energies. If your indoor plants are withering and dying, then the house is having bad omens because these omens are affecting the plants. However, ensure that you have placed the plants in the right place, where there it can get adequate sunshine, fresh air, the right temperature and humidity, and is watered when required. If all this is done, and there are not insects or diseases that the plant is suffering from, then it is best to find out the bad omen and take appropriate action.

What are the basic principles of Feng Shui?

The basic principles of feng shui are the five elements of nature, which are the water, fire, earth, metal and wood, the balance of nature, that is, the Yin and Yang, the solar system and other natural forces and energies.

On what basis are the principles of Feng Shui applied?

Feng Shui has been formulated and derived from the calculations, analysis and theories that are described in Yijing or I Ching, which is an ancient Chinese book of divination. The principles of feng shui are based on the balance of life to maintain peace and harmony. This is through the forces of Yin and Yang, which helps in balancing the five major elements of nature, which are fire, earth, water, metal, and wood. It also takes into consideration the type of relationship between the natural forces.

Can Feng Shui resolve problems like a bankruptcy, relationship issues and so on?

Feng shui can only promote energy it cannot completely cure anything. If the forces of nature, the star alignment and the placements of astrological forces are all wrong feng shui cannot help. Also, not everything is curable and so it is important to know that feng shui is a form of lifestyle that helps in harnessing energy. In cases of problems, it is best to resort to practical measures as well like perhaps shifting or moving to a different location. feng shui however can help.

Is the art of Feng Shui only applicable to houses or can it be applied to workplaces too?

No, as you can see from reading this book, feng shui is a form of lifestyle that comes from analyzing the energy around us and therefore it can be applicable to homes, workplaces, gardens and practically any location.

Do wind chimes a form an integral part of Feng Shui?

Wind chimes do play an important role in the applications of feng shui, however, this is true only if they are made of metal and not of anything else. They also need to be placed in correct directions and not following these could lead to adverse problems, as it will attract bad luck.

Is Feng Shui associated with Taoism or Buddhism?

Feng shui is not related to Buddhism or Taoism. Feng shui is considered to be a way of living that comes about from analyzing the energy that various objects emit.

Chapter 20
Feng Shui Tips for Beginners

A lot of the tips that have been provided in this book may be a little too advanced for someone that has simply no knowledge whatsoever regarding feng shui and where it comes from.

Hence, in order to help the people that are perhaps not as familiar with the art of feng shui as those more experienced with this practice, this chapter contains a list of tips that will help them to get the basic of feng shui down. These basic tips can be applied without putting in too much effort.

Clean Your House Out

One of the biggest roadblocks to feng shui is a cluttered home. The energies nexuses present within your home are just not able to spread their power along the pathways as efficiently if your home is cluttered. A messy house essentially invites negative energies and stagnations, which is probably why people with cluttered homes are so anxious all of the time.

Hence, cleaning up your house is essential to feng shui, and can be considered the single most important rule of basic feng shui. However, cleaning up may seem easy enough on paper but it can actually be quite difficult to do in actual practice.

This is because most people just can't tell the difference between things they need and things they don't. They just are not able to differentiate, and these things pile up to cause clutter.

A general rule to figure out if something should be in your home or not is to question whether the thing in question is something you love or not. This is important. Apart from the necessities, your home should only have things that you love within it.

Anything you don't love is going to have a negative energy, and you are naturally going to want to throw it away!

Natural Air and Natural Light

Feng shui is deeply rooted in nature, as the energies it derives its power from are naturally present in the physical world. This means that the more nature you include in your home, the more effective feng shui practices are going to become!

This is a huge problem because we tend to forego natural options as far as air and light are concerned. Too many homes favor light bulbs and air conditioners over windows, and this results in negative energy becoming prevalent within your home.

Instead of an air conditioner, open a window and if the air outside is polluted use some air purifying plants or air purifying machine to make the air that is permeating your home as clean as possible.

Additionally, the light that comes into your home during the day should be as pure as possible, which means that you must favor natural light to the best of your abilities.

Additionally, you should consider using full spectrum lights at night where there is no option for natural light. These full spectrum lights are a lot more natural than light bulbs and will facilitate the spreading of positive energy within your home.

Create an Energy Map

This is an essential part of basic feng shui. By creating an energy map, you will be able to define what parts of your home are dedicated to which area of your life which is very important. Without an energy map you will be essentially blindly placing random objects across your home and hoping that these objects purify your energy!

I would recommend using the traditional energy map that is prescribed in ancient feng shui. This map involves drawing a diagram of your room with the entrance at the bottom.

The lower portion of your room defines your career, the top left defines wealth, the top right defines creativity. Additionally, the bottom left corner of your room will decide the presence of positive people in your life, while the opposite corner is going to facilitate spiritual growth.

Once you have ascertained which portion of you room defines which aspect of your life it is going to become a lot easier to apply the techniques of feng shui. Keeping yourself informed is an important part of the process because doing it right can really end up changing your life!

Maintain a Balance of the Elements

In an upcoming chapter in this book, I am going to describe to you the presence of elements within certain colors and how these colors are going to help balance the energies in your life. A balanced elemental system in your room is going to result in your energies achieving equilibrium. This is going to allow you to live a more balanced life!

You already know which corners of your home pertain to which aspects of your life. It is important to ensure that you do not favor any one aspect more than the other. If wealth is your focus, place a little emphasis on the wealth corner of your home but try not to go overboard.

This is because going overboard results in a severe imbalance of energies. Heavily favoring the wealth corner of your home may make you rich for a period, but this wealth will be tainted with misfortune. As a result, you will end up wealthy but severely unhappy because your energies would not be aligned.

Hence, do not favor any one section of your home over the other. Focus on every aspect of your home and your life and eventually you will find an equilibrium in every single aspect of your life as well!

Use your Birth Element

One of the most important things that you can do in feng shui is to use your birth element. Finding your birth element is really easy and can be done by any experienced feng shui practitioner.

Once you have discovered your birth element, you must realize that you have truly unlocked the great secret to making feng shui work for you. Adorning your home in your birth element is any excellent way to balance out your energies and make it so that your life begins to repair itself.

If you are wondering how you can use your birth element to decorate your home, it is important that you realize that birth elements correspond to color as well. For example, if your birth element is fire, you can adorn your home with the colors of fire, and your energies will begin to align themselves automatically.

However, keep in mind that the focus on your birth element should come after you have balanced the energies in all of the corners of your home. If you don't, the aforementioned negative energies will begin to permeate the place you live.

Apply Your Kua and Direction

One basic aspect of feng shui is that everybody is born with a lucky number, or Kua, as well as a lucky direction. These two often go hand in hand.

Once again, you can use an experienced feng shui trainer or practitioner to help discover your Kua. If your lucky number is, for example, two, then your lucky direction is the southeast. This means that everything important in your life should face southeast if you want to experience success in that activity.

You can start by putting your desk in that direction. This will help you to align yourself with your specific meridian of universal energy. This energy will give you strength and intelligence as you work, resulting in improved performance on your part.

Additionally, you should consider facing your bed in your lucky direction as well. This will result in a deep and restful sleep and might even help you to sleep less while getting more energetic!

Doing so can also help you get very vivid dreams, and in a lot of situations people have reported that it helped them have lucid dreams.

Pay Attention to Your Energies

Once all of the groundwork has finally been set, the only thing that you have left to do is to remain alert of the energies within your home.

Remember, there is a triad of energy nexuses within your home. This triad is formed of your bedroom, your kitchen, and your bathroom, which are incidentally the most important parts of your home as well!

Be very mindful of the energies that are permeating these three areas of your house. Applying feng shui techniques will align your energies, but the pathways and meridians that you are purifying very rarely ever remain unmoving. Rather, these energy pathways tend to move quite a lot.

Be aware of the energies within your home. If you start feeling the presence of negative energies, act on what your intuition is telling you. Even if you have applied feng shui techniques to ward of negative energies, if you feel negative energies permeating your home try to find out where they could be coming from.

More often than not, these negative energies will have been coming through a gap in your feng shui, and this is easy to fix if you catch it early on.

Chapter 21

Applying the Elements through Color

A lot of people tend to get confused when the elements are spoken of. If your birth element is fire, how are you supposed to adorn your home with it? Are you supposed to set your house on fire?

Obviously not, but fire is still what your home should represent. You can represent the elements in your home using color, and this chapter is all about this particular aspect of feng shui. The colors that represent each element are described here in detail, along with how these colors can be applied to your home.

Wood

Wood is perhaps the earthiest of all of the elements that you can decorate your home with, apart from earth itself of course. The color that most people tend to associate with wood is brown, or dark brown to be precise.

However, what a lot of people don't know is that another color that you can use in order to boost the effects of wood within your home is green. Wood is part of plant life, which means that the entire green spectrum corresponds and obeys the commands of wood.

By decorating your home in brown and green colors, you are going to derive all of the benefits that are usually seen from the presence of wood within homes.

These benefits include improving your overall health as well as improving your family life. If you are experiencing domestic issues at home, such as fights with your spouse or children who don't respect you, try to get as much green and brown into your life as possible.

Green stimulates growth and vibrancy, and wood stimulates maturity and roundedness. Both of these aspects are very important to the modern family, and should encourage the use of green and brown in the modern home.

Fire

Out of all of the elements in this chapter, fire is the one with perhaps the most colors associated with it. The most obvious colors are red and orange, and it is certainly true that these colors pertain to fire and stimulate fire-like qualities in an individual and home. However, there are a lot more colors that stimulate fire in your home as well.

Yellow is one of the more obvious colors too. However, a lot of people don't know that the colors pink and purple also correspond to fire.

Using fire in your home, not as your birth element but as a part of your overall feng shui can stimulate happiness during gatherings. These colors stimulate a sense of protectiveness among people within the home, and this ends up giving way to the most enjoyable of family and friends gatherings!

If you are the kind of person that entertains a lot, consider bedecking the south end of your home in as many fire related colors as possible. This is going to ensure that your gatherings go well, and will make people want to come to your home again and again.

Earth

Earth and wood share a lot of common aspects. Both of these elements are earthy, earth more so obviously, but they also share a common color: brown.

Wood tends to correspond to a darker brown, however. Earth, on the other hand, can be represented by using a lighter brown. Additionally, you can represent earth in the feng shui of your home by using colors such as light yellow as well. Try to use colors that correspond to the color of sand too.

The color of the sand is very important. All of the ancient mysticism of Arabia came from sandy colored dunes, and this is no coincidence. Applying sandy colors, in particular, can boost wisdom within the inhabitants of the home!

You can also use earth to facilitate family gatherings much in the same way as fire. Earth is a very accommodating element and shares a lot with several other elements. Wood and fire are both individualistic elements, but it is the accommodating nature of Earth that allows them to be intrinsically linked to one another.

Hence, if you are looking for a bond with someone, use light brown and light yellow colors in that part of your home.

Metal

Metal is the coldest and most remote of all of the elements. However, this remoteness must not be confused as isolation, as it is a very loving element as well. It is just not as good at showing it as earth is, nor is it as passionate as fire!

Many people find it surprising that metal is a very nurturing element. This is reflected in the colors that represent it. White, the purest of all colors, is usually representing metal, as is gray which is known for being muted and regal among other things.

The benefits of using metal, particularly when white is used to represent it, are numerous. You can use these colors to boost creativity within your home.

White can be applied to the northern corner of your home in order to stimulate your creativity. This is particularly useful if you are an artist and are suffering from a creative block!

You should also consider placing your children's play area in that section of the house and decorating it with white furniture and decorations. This will help boost your children's creativity while playing, which is scientifically proven to boost the intelligence of a child and help them grasp abstract concepts more easily!

Water

This is the calmest element among all of the elements described in this chapter. This is probably why the color that pertains to it most often is blue. Blue is the most serene color, as it is known to boost within people a sense of calmness and contentment.

Another color that is often associated with water is black! This is because water is completely incompatible with metal, which means that the color pertaining to this element must be in direct opposition to the color pertaining to metal!

You can obviously not use metal and water together, but you can use water in conjunction with wood. Water can act as a support to wood, offering it growth as it boosts the love in your home and helps make your family a tighter-knit unit.

You can also use water to boost your wealth by placing as much blue in the wealth corner of your home as possible. Water is the color of wealth, surprisingly enough. This should tell you that wealth is very abundant in the world, just like water is. This means that all you have to do to become wealthy is to reach out and take the wealth that you want!

Veronica Fujii

Chapter 22

Applying the Elements through Shapes

A slightly more abstract concept from color is the expression of elements through shapes. These elements are not restricted to one aspect of the physical world and can be expressed in a variety of ways.

The great thing about using shapes to express elements is that you can combine these shapes with colors to get double the elemental boost. You could also use neutral colors and still get the same amount of elemental boost as you would if you had used the colors pertaining to these elements.

Wood

As you already know, wood is a loving element, but also has strong mental strength. This makes it quite similar to earth but not as pliable, and if you want to get the most out of this element, you should use rectangular shapes as much as possible.

This goes quite beautifully with the various ways in which wood can be used in the modern home. A coffee table will most likely be rectangular, as will most of the wood based items that you would be using in your home. You can combine these with different colors to get multiple effects!

Fire

Fire is a very passionate but abrasive element. This abrasion helps make you more aggressive in a good way. However, it is often difficult to think of what shape would pertain to this particular element. In order to figure out the shape, you need to actually look at a fire.

A fire in a fireplace can usually fit into one very obvious shape: a triangle. Hence, if you want as much fire based energy in your home, the best shape that you can use is a triangle. Try to combine this shape with the color of fire in order to get the best results.

Earth

You already know that earth and wood share a lot of similarities in color. These similarities extend to the shapes that represent each of these elements as well.

The shape for wood is a rectangle. The shape for earth is a square, which is very similar in shape to a rectangle. Hence, you can combine shades of brown with rectangles and squares in your home to get a very earthy and woody feel, boosting love, maturity, and acceptance within your home. It is the perfect cure for any domestic issue!

Metal

The shape of metal is perhaps the least obvious, and this is because it does not pertain to any obvious physical aspect of metal. However, this is because we usually look at processed and shape metal. To ascertain the shape of metal, we would need to look at metal in its original form.

Metal, in its original form, looks like nuggets of silver and gray. These nuggets conform to a single shape: round. Hence, incorporating round shapes into your homes is an excellent way to boost the presence of metal in your home. Combine these shapes with white and gray colors for better effects.

Water

The shape of water is perhaps the most obvious out of all of the elements in this list. Water is often seen in waves, which means that naturally the shape that best suits water is wavy.

Wavy shapes can be combined with blue, of course. However, it is also highly recommended that you combine these shapes with green and dark brown. This is going to give you the combined effect of water and wood.

Water is plentiful; wood is solid. The combination of these two characteristics can result in a long and happy family life for you.

Chapter 23

How to Enhance Energy in Feng Shui Corners

You might not be wondering what exactly you can do in order to boost the energy of the corners within your home. You've been told about the elements, but how can you use this information in an efficient and effective way?

The best way to do this is by using energy enhancers. This chapter is all about what energy enhancers you can use in order to get the most out of your feng shui.

Colors

You have been told about how colors pertain to the various elements. However, you should not feel restricted by these elements. You should instead use the colors you love outside of the important corners of your home!

Colors are a visual delight. The presence of colors in the world gives way to such intense beauty that it can have an actual, measurable effect on the human mind.

Hence, it is very important that you add colors where you want them. If you boost the amount of color within your home, you are going to find that it will improve your outlook on life, which is actually a direct result of the feng shui!

Try to be as diverse with the colors that you use as possible. These colors are an important part of your home life, so try to incorporate them into as many parts of your home as possible, even your garden. You can use colors to bring color to your summer parties in your yard!

Mirrors

Mirrors hold great power in the world of feng shui. This is because it is believed that mirrors are the keys to our souls, that in looking at ourselves through them we see our truest representation. This is unlike a picture, where the representation is separate from our actual selves.

You can use mirrors to fill up areas where you don't have furniture or even fill up a wall in a section of your home. For example, you can put a mirror up in the creativity section of your home in order to look upon your own reflection whenever you feel as though you are going through a creative block.

This will show you that your creativity is within yourself and is not something you need to look for elsewhere! It is recommended that you avoid foggy or distorted mirrors, and that you avoid putting mirrors in your bedroom.

A Well Lit Home

Nothing spoils the flow of chi within your home like darkness. You should try as much as possible to bring natural light into your home. Additionally, it is important that you keep an option for dim lighting when your mood suits it.

Sometimes, there is too much artificial light, and this interrupts the flow of chi between energy nexuses in your home. In order to address this problem, it is important that you use dimmer switches with your lights. This will allow you to incorporate more natural light into your home.

You can also have lights facing upwards if your room is small. This will help to create the illusion of a larger room, much in the same way that mirrors do. Downward facing lighting for larger rooms can also help to make the room feel less empty and cozier than it actually is.

Art

Art is one of the most beautiful forms of human expression. By incorporating just a single painting into your home you are going to really boost the level of creativity and content for the people you are living with. This is because they will finally have an outlet of some sort that will help them achieve peace.

Try to make sure that the art that you put up in your home is something that everybody feels comfortable about. If a painting you have put up makes someone you are living with uneasy, it is better to take that painting down. This is because the effect of the painting will be reduced by the negative energy that this person's uneasiness would be emitting.

As long as you don't have negative energy tainting your paintings, including them in your home will make it vibrant, exciting and full of life and will really boost the effectiveness of feng shui.

Crystals

Crystals are powerful tools that are used by the vast majority of feng shui practitioners and for good reason. They are incredibly regulators of energy and help make it so that any discrepancies in the flow of energy in your home becomes less prominent.

Crystals work as filters in a way. Your energy within your home is a lot like coffee. Sometimes the coffee needs to be filtered in order to remove lumps and make it smoother and more palatable. However, crystals work the other way too. If the energy within your home is watered down or too light in some way, crystals can magnify the energy and make it stronger as a result.

Use crystals to decorate your home so that you know that you have objects that are regulating the flow of chi energy in case your feng shui becomes insufficient.

Wind Chimes

A little-known fact about chi is that it is intrinsically linked with sound. The more sound that is being generated within your home, the more chi that will be generated as a result.

However, this can cause problems. If your children are noisy, or if loud music is frequently played in your home you will find that the amount of energy within your home will rise to stifling levels. As a result, your home might end up forming blockages in its energy pathways because it will not be able to handle so much energy.

The best solution for this is a wind chime. Wind chimes provide calming sounds that can regulate the chi that is produced due to excess noise within the home. The energy that the wind chimes themselves produce is serene and does not require any inordinate amount of regulation itself.

Pets and Plants

Chi is generated in enormous amounts from things that you unconditionally take care of. This includes plants and pets. Keep in mind that you must take very good care of your plants and pets if you want the desired results. If you keep them happy they are going to emanate warm, positive chi for your entire home.

However, if you do not take care of any plants or pets that you adopt, you are going to end up getting a lot of negative chi in your home. These animals and plants have feelings, and not taking care of these feelings ends up releasing negative energy that can end up wreaking havoc with your feng shui.

Additionally, avoid all kinds of dried plants and potpourri. These are not vibrant and only end up collecting dust. However, fake plants made of silk can be used as long as they are thrown out after they are no longer lustrous.

Natural Objects

Apart from plants and pets, you can also incorporate natural objects into the feng shui of your home. These natural objects can be objects such as shells from the beach or a stone that you picked up while walking in nature.

These objects emit excellent chi energy, but make sure that they do not end up becoming clutter in your home otherwise they would end up creating negative energy. Try to arrange them in an attractive manner, and never let them gather dust.

You can also place objects in your garden that would attract wildlife, such as a bird bath. The wildlife that would end up getting attracted to these features would bring great chi to your home. Try your best to make sure that the water in the bird bath does not go foul as this would end up creating negative chi.

Water Features

Water features are great because water is considered in feng shui to be intrinsically linked to wealth. Water is perfect for practically every corner of your home and is considered the most universally compatible element as far as feng shui goes. The only thing it is not compatible with is fame. Water is such a common element that putting it in the fame corner of your home will end up offsetting most of the other elements in that corner.

In order to derive the fantastic benefits that water has to offer, it is highly recommended that you get as many water features in your home as possible. These water features are a great way to boost the chi in your home as long as you don't let the water go foul. Try to make the water features wooden or colored blue. This will mix water with different elements, the combination being the source of great power!

Fire Features

Fire features are less common than water features, mostly because we tend to use heaters rather than fire to warm our homes now. However, heaters are not compatible with feng shui, whereas fire is.

Incorporating a fireplace into your home is not the only fire feature that will help, however. You can also incorporate tiki lanterns. The great thing about tiki lanterns is that they are safer and less expensive than fireplaces, making them a great choice for incorporating feng shui on a budget.

It may seem somewhat costly, but incorporating fire features into your home will actually end up facilitating a more peaceful family life for you. This is certainly worth it if you are the kind of person that wants peace and quiet at home!

Mobiles

A mobile is any object that swings and rotates when the wind hits it. These objects are excellent because they offer chi energy an entryway into your home.

Chi often moves in the direction of the wind, and the movement of the mobiles when they come into contact with the wind acts as a sort of beckoning gesture to chi.

You can also use wind dancers, which are like wind chimes without the noise, in this manner. Overall, these items can prove to be very useful to you while you are attempting to boost the presence of chi in your home, and can come together to make your feng shui a lot more effective.

Chapter 24
Feng Shui Tip for Your Purse

The purse is the source of all money as far as feng shui is concerned. Hence, there is a certain etiquette that can be applied to your purse that can be derived from the feng shui philosophy. This philosophy is actually quite intuitive, and if you apply it to your life, you will find that your wealth will begin to increase. Hence, here are ten tips that will help you boost your wealth by taking better care of your purse:

Stop Using Your Purse as a Trash Can

A major mistake that women make with their purposes is that they treat them like trash cans. They tend to dump everything into their purses from chips packets to used tissues, and this really spoils the energy of the purse.

A purse is supposed to be where you put your money, not where you deposit trash. Once you stop using your purse in this manner, you are going to find that a lot of the money problems you were facing will be gone in the blink of an eye!

Keep Your Purse Elevated

Another common mistake that women make regarding their purse is that they keep it on the floor, even in the bathroom! This seriously affects the energy of your purse and makes it so that your money will be affected in a negative way.

Think of it this way, a man never puts his wallet on the floor! The place where you put your money should be treated with respect, as money is what you are going to use to survive.

Hence, keep your purse off the floor at all costs, especially in the bathroom where you should hang it on a coat hanger.

Respect the Change

Change is money just like all other money. Even if you don't intend to use it, don't just throwing it into your purse is one of the worst things that you can do as it is disrespectful of money.

Instead of tossing your coins into your purse, try to place them in a pouch. Your purse probably has lots of different pockets, and putting your coins into these pockets will help you in the long run.

You will be surprised at how much your change is worth! Soon you might be able to eat lunch with the change that you have saved up.

Fill Your Purse with Useful Items

You need to change the way you look at your purse. Instead of treating it like repository for garbage, you should treat it as an all-purpose emergency kit not just for yourself but for everyone else.

Keep emergency supplies in your purse, and also keep some extra money in there. Try not to spend this money, instead just keep it in there for emergencies. This will help your purse become a place of secret wealth which is going to be very helpful in the long run.

Bedeck Your Purse with Charms

Feng shui is all about the power of elements. The power of water as far as wealth is concerned is well known, which means that if you associate water based charms with your purse you can boost the amount of wealth in your life.

These charms have to be wavy and blue, both color and shape being representative of water. Additionally, you can change the color of the charm from blue to black if you prefer. Black is just as water aspected as blue and is obviously a lot more stylish.

Buy Practical Purses

Your purse is one of the most important items in your life. This means that when you buy a purse, you must buy one that is compatible with you.

It is pretty common to want to buy a purse that is stylish. However, this style is going to do nothing for your personal feng shui unless the purse is compatible with you.

This means that your purse should be comfortable and should sit well on your shoulder. Additionally, your purse should contain little compartments that you can use for small objects. Remember, your purse first and foremost needs to be functional.

Create a Spot in Your Purse for Your Keys

This is part of your attempt to clean out clutter from your purse. Remember, clutter is the death of feng shui. If your purse has large amounts of clutter in it, you will find that you will not have a lot of money, or at least not as much money as you are supposed to have.

By using a little hook or a pocket for your keys, you will also be a lot safer if you need to get into your car as quickly as possible.

Organize Your Wallet

Another important part of keeping your purse clean is to clear the clutter from your wallet. This obviously means taking everything that doesn't need to be there out.

However, another important part of clearing the clutter from your wallet is arranging your money. Don't just crumple up the notes into your wallet, try to keep them as neatly as possible.

It will also really help if you arrange the money according to the value of each note. This will align your financial energies and will also help you know just how much you have in your wallet at any given time.

Get a Purse in a Wealth Color

Blue and black are the colors of water, which means that they are also the colors of wealth. Getting a purse in these colors will really help you to boost the wealth in your life.

However, you can also get purses in the colors of the wealth color you were assigned at birth. This color is yours and yours alone. In order to discover it, all you have to do is approach an expert at feng shui, or someone who teaches feng shui.

Getting a purse in this color will greatly boost your wealth energies, which in turn will result in you getting wealthier in no time.

Get a Purse that you Love

The most important thing about feng shui is liking your environment. Otherwise, your negative energies will taint the environment and make it less effective than it should be.

Hence, the best thing that you can do to boost your wealth based energies is to buy a purse that you love. Try to make it as practical as possible, but at the end of the day the only thing that really matters is whether you like the purse that you are using or not.

Veronica Fujii

Conclusion

I thank you once again for purchasing this book, and I hope you lead a life of prosperity after reading it. Feng shui has been practiced for thousands of years although the results aren't instantaneous. However, there is a significant change in fortune noticed over time.

You will experience a burst of optimism, and feel motivated and relaxed. Provided, you do not give up on the process and wait for the positive energy to emerge. You will need to take the first step in order to attain a state of balance. Once you notice a change, you will motivate yourself and keep yourself energized and relieved.

It is always recommended you take it slow, one room at a time and not to try too much in little time.

I hope you make use of the ideas mentioned in this book and increase your house's feng shui value. In fact, use the ideas mentioned for the garden and the children's room as well and help the science improve your overall existence.

Once you get the hang of it, you will start to adopt it all around and improve your living. You can also recommend it to a friend as having company will always up your enthusiasm, and you will start investing more time and energy into it.

Printed in Great Britain
by Amazon.co.uk, Ltd.,
Marston Gate.